Slow Car Fast

The Millennial Mantra Changing Car Culture for Good

Ryan K. ZumMallen

A Carrara Book
Published by Carrara Media, LLC

Cover illustration by Aaron Sanchez

https://www.carrarabooks.com/slow-car-fast

ISBN:
978-0-578-54970-5 (Paperback)
978-0-578-56038-0 (Mobi for Kindle)
978-0-578-56037-3 (EPUB for eReader)
978-0-578-56466-1 (PDF)

Manufactured in the United States of America

First Edition: July 2019

For Claire.

Acknowledgments

First of all, my heartfelt thanks to the hundreds of people who allowed me access to their passion and their lives, paying with their time and in some cases their money to help make this project a reality. There were many people who did not have to return phone calls, emails or direct messages, and then did not have to say yes to a writer they'd never heard of, but decided to anyway. This would not be possible without their abundant generosity.

To friends and family who offered feedback and expertise, I cannot express what your guidance means to me. Andrew Veis, Brian Roberts and Adam Anderson for answering all of my questions and then answering all those I didn't know to ask. Alan Schaefer and Victoria Parsons Gracie for keeping me focused and on the right path. Aaron Montan, Russell Conroy, Shannon Doherty, J.J. Fiddler, Erica Brenes, Jason Douglas and Chuck Lilliard for their valuable feedback. Kelly Conroy for the first critical eye, a crucial boost when I needed one and some much-needed medicine too.

And to my parents. Dana Sunderland and my stepfather Todd Stark for their steadfast encouragement. David ZumMallen for laying the foundation for this book and my career many years ago, without even knowing it, and all the years of support since.

I would be lost without Sarah Bennett, who fearlessly attacked a new topic like she'd known it for years and vastly improved this project in all the ways I expected, and in so many ways that I didn't. The same goes for Aaron Sanchez, who blew me away with every concept and every sketch and every finished draft. I have no idea how you do it, but I'm so glad you do.

Finally, to Nikol. My inspiration, my partner in love and life. Everything I know about making a plan, and following through, I learned by watching all of the impossible things you accomplish each day. You believed in me and encouraged me and made time for me when it would have been more sensible to do the opposite. This project, and all the ones before it, and all the ones to come, happened because you are in my life. I am a million miles beyond lucky to share this ride with you.

Table of Contents

Chapter I: Does Fast Matter?

Gordon stiffens the arms in his blue designer jacket, dark eyes locked ahead behind polarized sunglasses with each hair arranged neatly coiffed in place, belying the fact that he is about to punch me in the kidneys. He tightens his grip on the steering wheel, straightens the car, and punches the gas pedal. We're inside his brand new toy, an insane vehicle that looks more like a spaceship than a car. It's called the McLaren Senna. It has enormous vents, dramatic angles and sits just centimeters off the ground. It has 800 horsepower—about four times more than the average car on sale today—and distributes it with the fury of the gods. In my decade of writing and reporting on the automotive industry, I've never rode shotgun in anything faster.

Vision blurs. My feet lift off the floor, my hips levitate and my stomach begins to float up into my throat. The road, cars, trees and sky blend together and then cease to exist. It all becomes one whooshing wave of universe and none of it matters. The entire outside world is deduced into two categories: Senna and Not Senna. The roads are full of fast cars like Mustangs and Camaros, and in most parts of the U.S. there are a handful of supercars like Ferraris and Porsches lurking around. And then there are hypercars. The term had to be invented when things like the Senna started showing up. It reaches 110 mph in an instant and then coasts to a cruising highway speed. It's all over in three seconds. "That was about eight-tenths," Gordon says. This is not his first McLaren. He is 25.

Gordon prefers to be anonymous. On Instagram he's known by the pseudonym @sbp_one, where he posts photos of his vast car collection to thousands of followers. But he never reveals his face or name. He agrees to let me tag along under the condition his identity stays secret. The attention can be overwhelming. Gordon has grown used to onlookers stopping in the street and pulling out smartphones. Some peer hard into the windows in case there's a celebrity inside. During our drive, a Volkswagen pulls alongside the

Senna and slows to match its speed like they're tethered together. A passenger in the VW hangs half his body out the window, clutching a digital camera to snap off some moving shots. Gordon smiles and waves. Sometimes, people follow him home. When it gets especially bad, Gordon will schedule meetings with local photographers and tell them to invite friends. That way they can get all the shots they want in one showing. He understands that they are excited and enthusiastic about these kinds of cars. He's the same way.

Gordon fell in love with speed for good around the age of 15. As his family built a thriving business, he lusted after cars in magazines, researched and debated them for hours on end on the Internet. By the time he turned 19 he had assumed control over his family's fleet of rare and exotic supercars, in charge of their maintenance and upkeep but also decision-making over which ones to buy and when to sell. Gordon is a practicing engineer but his fleet management hobby could be a full-time job in itself. He obsesses over minor details. For the Senna he wanted the exterior coated in blue paint. Not just any blue. Gordon wanted a shade of blue that would leap off the car. He tried to describe his vision as "an exploding blue." Then, "a volcano blue." He had hour-long conversations with McLaren's head of paint. He sent ten samples to the factory in England. They sent him three back. "I try not to be high-maintenance," he told me. "But I knew what I wanted." Gordon eventually picked one and named it Presidio Blue, after a Spanish fort near the ocean.

Gordon and his family are not typical car collectors. They manage a warehouse to house their fleet and own multiple cars from a wide array of automakers. But their closest relationship is with McLaren. The company launched an effort to take over the supercar market in 2011 with the plucky little MP4-12C sports car. Gordon bought a black one. A few years later McLaren announced the radical P1, an alien-molded supercar with an all-electric hybrid mode and a punishingly sonorous engine note. Gordon bought an orange one. Back then, fewer than five years into its mission, McLaren was young enough that a relatively unknown buyer could walk into a dealer and pick out their car unannounced. Even a P1. But soon, McLaren had earned the right to choose its customers. So in 2018 a select group of lucky souls were presented with the opportunity to purchase one in a limited run of 500 hypercars that McLaren declared would put all others to shame. It cost $1 million. They released no other details about the car—no images, no engine specs and no top speed. It didn't have a name. McLaren called Gordon. He said yes.

Even in the eclectic world of hypercar collecting the Senna is an odd duck. It looks like if a catfish had gills on every inch of its body. McLaren made no effort to make it comfortable. There is essentially no sound-deadening material to speak of. The car's parts were selected because they either make it lighter or faster. The engine is 15 inches behind your head and it screams directly into your ears. Any crack in the road causes the carbon fiber dashboard to bounce and jostle. The race-tuned suspension chooses not to cushion any of it out. There is a constant hum that never goes away. Nearly everything is higher than you are. Family station wagons pass by like double-decker buses. In the bottom half of the door, from your ankle to your knee, there is a window looking down on the outside pavement. The McLaren Senna is less a car and more an experiment to test the limits of sensory overload on the human brain. And that's before it accelerates. When Gordon punches it, my head thuds against the soft padding at the top of the lightweight bucket seat barely holding my body, and all of its insides, in place. "What is the point of having a car this fast on public roads?" I ask myself that question later. There isn't time inside the Senna. All you can do is look straight ahead and smile.

Cars have gotten fast. And fast has gotten easy. The Senna is in a rare league of hypercars, but there are thousands of ways to get your speed kicks these days. You don't need to own the latest Ferrari, or Porsche, or even BMW M car to experience the kind of thrill that was once only attainable to the extremely lucky few. Technologies like turbocharging, direct injection, all-wheel drive, traction control and, yes, electrification, have made it relatively simple for automakers to shoehorn whatever level of performance they so choose into any vehicle. There are muscle cars with 750 horsepower, station wagons with zero-to-60 times under four seconds and SUVs that lap the Nürburgring in eight minutes flat[1]. Car culture has reached a saturation of speed. If everything is fast, does that mean that nothing is fast? Does fast even matter?

When the car comes back to cruising speed I let out a laugh that would be embarrassing in virtually any other situation. But in the Senna it feels natural. The car is simply capable of warping your perception of speed. And it is not alone. Along with its peers—giants like the Porsche 918 Spyder and Ferrari LaFerrari, the Bugatti Veyron and the Pagani Huayra and Koenigsegg Agera—it has ushered in the age of the hypercar. By the time you open the butterfly doors skyward, step over the massive carbon fiber door sill and re-accustom your senses to the natural world there is only one remaining thought on your mind: How the hell did we get here?

*

I met Gordon for the first time earlier that morning, on the grass-lined sidewalk outside a small nondescript warehouse behind an automatic metal gate. He had been referred to me by a mutual acquaintance who knew of my interest in the hypercar world, and thought Gordon would be a good person to provide an inside look. I wanted to know more exotic car owners. For most of us, the occasional fleeting glimpse at a racetrack or local car show is as close as we'll get to inhabiting this world. Few things appear more glamorous than pulling up in a vehicle that's lusted over by a drooling crowd. For many it's a dream to one day own a car that inspires dropped jaws. The truth is that most of the people who pull up in those vehicles don't own a car like that—they own several cars like that. Sometimes, they own dozens. Gordon is one of those guys.

Before our meeting, I hadn't been able to find any information about Gordon. Even after learning his name and occupation, my Internet searches were fruitless. Some people are apparently very good at staying mysterious. I arrived knowing only that we were attending an auto show in a Senna with 100 miles on its odometer. But as I walked up the sidewalk toward the warehouse and Gordon stepped out to greet me everything changed.

"Hey, thanks for coming!" he called with a warm smile and a handshake that rippled the muscles in my forearm. Then he introduced me to three friends standing in the driveway, two young men and a woman, each in their mid-20s, smiling and friendly but not exactly sure what to make of this strange visitor who parked his 12-year-old Mitsubishi a block down the road. One described the 100,000-mile Lotus Elise that he both races and drives on his daily commute. Another recently bought a Porsche Cayman GT4 on a whim to establish credit (he'd previously bought all his supercars in cash). They joked about the silliest questions they get asked at gas stations and the made-up careers they offer when asked what they do for a living. (Most common: drug dealer.) They showed me a secret text chain where a circle of fellow insiders send unreleased photos and information on upcoming cars. It's titled "DNS," or Do Not Share. I'm sworn to secrecy on the contents and members of the chat. This is a different world. "Is this your first McLaren?" one asked me.

Gordon invited everyone inside. The outside of the warehouse consists only of a bare building façade, a small entrance door to the left and a garage door to the right. There's no indication that anyone visits on a regular basis. When Gordon opened the door and lead us inside I expected the interior of the building to match its unadorned exterior. Instead it's a car collector playground. To the left, a murderer's row of supercar heavyweights: a Porsche Carrera GT, a Ford GT and a Shelby Cobra alongside one another, each one an iconic and transformational vehicle in its own right that defined their respective eras.

Swing around the full kitchen and entertaining area and the garage opens into another section of automotive greatness. Here, a small alcove houses another Carrera GT and another Ford GT. Faced by an Aston Martin V12 Vantage, a Ferrari 360 Challenge Stradale, an Audi R8 and a classic C2 Corvette. There is a McLaren MP4-12C and a special edition McLaren MSO X—only 10 exist. A red Ferrari 275 GTB stares back at me with its 1960s attitude. And in the center of it all is the Senna, looking futuristic and extreme in its transcendent Presidio Blue, a new big-winged entry into the hall of fame. I'd been so overwhelmed, I'd almost forgotten about it.

Gordon fired up the Senna, his friends started the R8 and the Cayman GT4. His father, also joining us, slid into the 275 GTB. One by one we filed out of the driveway and headed for the local Cars and Coffee show as the garage door lowers closed behind us.

*

I started going to car shows as soon as I could drive. Whether it was the local Mustang meet or the annual Father's Day show on Rodeo Drive there weren't many gatherings in the Los Angeles area I didn't frequent on a regular basis. Pretty soon I was leaving my neighborhood every weekend, at first from my parents' house in the desert of Santa Clarita and later my college fraternity house in Long Beach, and traveling farther and farther from home. In the Southern California car scene there was no shortage of interesting cars to keep a teenager drooling, and you never knew what was going to show up. Eventually, it became less about wanting to see interesting cars and more about feeling like I needed to be there whenever possible.

Things accelerated in the mid-2000s. Flush with cash during a housing bubble that had not yet popped, car collectors in Southern California and especially Orange County started gobbling up exotic supercars in greater and greater numbers. Automakers began to greenlight ambitious models with larger production runs to feed the demand. Orange County became swollen with marques that were once exclusive like Aston Martins, Lamborghinis and Ferraris. Lots of Ferraris. A group of owners caught wind of a growing hot rod show in nearby Huntington Beach that took over a donut shop parking lot each Saturday morning. The members called themselves the Donut Derelicts. There were no rules, official times, assigned spots or awards—a novel concept back in the 1980s and 1990s.

But the location was too small to start rolling in with a gaggle of supercars. So the owners found their own spot and started rolling their exotics into the expansive parking lot at the Crystal Cove Shopping Center, an outdoor mall directly across the street from million-dollar views of the Pacific ocean. There was a Starbucks smack in the center and few of the other businesses were open early enough to complain about the crowds. Soon there were dozens of high-end exotic cars filling the main parking lot to capacity every Saturday, and tons of rare gems stashed away in the overflow spaces that stretched for about a quarter-mile in either direction. All for free and with sparkling blue water in the background.

Crystal Cove became too big too fast. The spots filled up by 7:00 a.m. and visitor spaces were gone shortly after. Lines for the Starbucks bathroom were unmanageable. Dealerships showed up to park unsold vehicles there for free publicity. Enthusiasts with cameras lined up at the exits to get footage of the rarest cars in the world pulling out onto public roads, often encouraging reckless behavior. For a time, I was regrettably among them. More than once I witnessed drivers who couldn't control their cars nearly lose it into the crowd.

In the end, the real death knell came from the most predictable place: rich homeowners. Those who lived in the hills above the shopping center and had paid top dollar for their ocean views did not appreciate being woken up every Saturday by whooping V12 engines and earth-rumbling V8s. Organizers issued notice that the show would be shutting down on October 2, 2006—my 22nd birthday. "Crystal Cove" evolved into Cars and Coffee Irvine a few miles up the road. And it inspired hundreds of similar weekly Cars and Coffee meets in parking lots across the country that still go on today. C&C Irvine lasted a few years before flaming out. Partly because the ambiance wasn't the same as the original, partly because the show's host Mazda tired of the security measures required. But perhaps the biggest reason is that car culture is ever-changing and people, especially young ones, start to look for the next thing. Gawking over bone-stock supercars was out, replaced by the rise of social media and online car culture. And on forums and Instagram pages and YouTube channels across the Internet, the next wave of automotive enthusiasm began to take shape.

*

One of the local Cars and Coffee meets that sprung up in Crystal Cove's wake is just miles from Gordon's garage. After a romp down the freeway we caravan into the lot and take up four spaces, the Senna and 275 GTB and

Cayman GT4 alongside one another. There are supercars here—out of the 100 or so cars in attendance maybe 15 could be considered exotic. But there's also a healthy contingent of old beach cruisers, classic Americana sedans and muscled-up sleepers. The crowd is a mixed group with plenty of children and a handful of young girls clutching stuffed animals. But for the most part attendees are older, with a good portion having rolled up in traditional American show cars. It's a fun meet, eccentric and not all that serious with interesting people who've come to know and care about each other over the past several years of Saturdays.

As he nestles his Senna into a primo spot, Gordon parks and presses the bright red Race button that lowers the car to its minimum height above the ground—all the better for pictures. He reaches overheard to pull the door handle, located on the ceiling, lifts his door to the sky and steps out into a crowd of onlookers. He immediately begins to shake hands with old friends, and entertain questions from those with smartphones in hand, in awe of the Millennial who just stepped out of a spaceship. Gordon handles queries like a seasoned pro. He points to his favorite features: the optional black carbon roof scoop; the translucent "S" logo on the rear wing that disappears in the right light; the cartoon of a bloodied Sonic the Hedgehog with a tire mark splashed across his body that Ayrton Senna famously had painted on his racecar to mark his domination of his Sega Genesis-backed rivals at Williams F1[2]. Gordon plans to have the logo painted on his car and added to his key fob. He proceeds to tell these stories and the meaning behind "Presidio Blue" about a thousand times, always smiling and happy to start from the beginning.

Owning a hypercar is tiring work. Gordon puts up with it because cars like the Senna offer something that nothing else can.

"To me it's all about a memorable experience," he said as we rumbled along. "That's what the Senna provides. It's pushed the boundaries of performance so much that it's compromised in other areas, like the noise and vibration. And that creates something special that sets it apart from other cars. It gives you something unique. You can have a special experience without going top speed. You don't need to be driving at ten-tenths to have fun."

We return to the garage and park the Senna, milling about between tens of millions of dollars of cars. Gordon and his family bring them out as much as possible but it's too much for any group to drive regularly. The majority of the cars sit and wait for their moment in the spotlight. And among the modern supercars there are only a handful that could be considered classics. So I am surprised when I ask Gordon if there is one vehicle he hasn't owned yet that entices him, and he answers with a car from before his time. Before he was born, even. It's a car that speaks to a generation before his. "Oh, a Ferrari F40," he said. "The right opportunity hasn't come. But that's the one. That's the one."

*

The march toward the age of the hypercar took its first step 30 years ago. In the early 1980s, the iconic sports car maker Porsche began flirting with a very dangerous idea. The company wanted to enter Group B, the no-holds-barred rally racing series known for sensational and dangerous driving within inches of vast European crowds. Porsche built an advanced all-wheel drive system that could send varying levels of power to the front or rear wheels depending on traction and acceleration—the better for Group B's surfaces from pavement to gravel, dirt and mud. But to enter the league, teams were required to sell a street-legal version of the car to the public. Porsche began preparations to pair its all-wheel-drive with a turbocharged engine and unleash it on the streets.

At the time, both all-wheel drive and turbocharging in sports cars was uncommon. Combining the two, and putting it in the hands of anyone with a check large enough, was a landmark moment. Porsche took a version of the flat-six engine from its champion racecars and slapped on two turbochargers. The first prototype debuted at the 1983 Frankfurt Motor Show[3]. The first production version debuted two years later, but it took another two years to actually begin building the car, now known by a single name: 959. It would never race in Group B, which was cancelled in 1986 after numerous crashes. The 959 instead built its own legacy with wins at the Paris-Dakar rally and the 24 Hours of Le Mans. But on the street, it had a challenger.

Four-hundred miles away in Maranello, Italy, the legendary founder of the most famous carmaker in the world had a request. A simple one, really. Enzo Ferrari, then 88, still the patriarch of the company that bore his name and reverently known as the Old Man, came to his engineers. "Build a car to be the best in the world," he said[4]. Barely one year later the finished product made its debut. It wore an almost unbelievable wedge shape, accentuated by Ferrari's signature *Rosso Corsa* red. In the engine compartment, covered by a clear plastic shield to dissipate heat and show off the goods inside, lied a 3.0-liter V8 engine with dual turbochargers. Rear-wheel drive only. It marked the 40th anniversary of Ferrari's founding. It was called the F40. It was to be built immediately.

The Ferrari and the Porsche had been developed on different timelines. They'd come to their production versions with different shapes, different technologies and different number of cylinders. But there were unmistakable similarities. Both the 959 and F40 marked the absolute apex of each brand's performance capabilities at the time. They were priced accordingly: $225,000 for the Porsche and $400,000 for the Ferrari. They both began production in 1987. Looking back, there is one statistical similarity that stands head and shoulders above the others. The Porsche 959 and Ferrari F40 were the first production cars to go 200 miles per hour.

This was a defining moment in performance car history. The mass production automobile had been around for about a century, and in the previous 100 years the barriers in top-speed performance had come gradually. In 1949 the Jaguar XK120 kicked off the post-war boom in car technology by listing a top speed of 120 mph[5]—hence its name. The years that followed saw a steady recalibration of that record every couple of years. Mercedes-Benz hit 150 mph in 1955. Aston Martin did 152 in 1959. In the 1960s, upstart Lamborghini and old-guard Ferrari traded the record a couple of times until 1982, when the Lamborghini Countach LP500 S landed a deciding blow at 182 mph. That was damn fast and still is today. (At the time it was probably faster than cars of that build quality should have been allowed—the Countach notoriously lifts its front axle at speed, reducing its grip and stability. In an ironic twist, its giant wing pushed the rear down, lifting the front even more[6].) But in the 23 years before 1982, the top speed production cars were capable of achieving had increased about 16 percent, a small margin.

That changed with the 959 and F40. Almost overnight there were two head-to-head challengers for the title of best car in the world that had blown by every previous contender. Just 30 years after the Aston Martin DB4, they'd both beaten its record top speed by roughly one-third. These were not just engineering marvels, or cultural touchstones that turned millions of youth into car nuts who obsessed over their over-engineered details. They were a sign to automakers around the world that the bar had been raised. The new achievable top speed number for production cars was 200 mph—and beyond.

It didn't take long for others to respond. Six years later the McLaren F1 reached 221 mph. In the 2000s hypercar-makers Koenigsegg and Bugatti traded punches: the CCR with 241, the Veyron with 253 and later 258, and finally the Agera RS with a whopping 277 mph. There is a fair amount of debate and hot air surrounding the capability of other contenders, methods for testing such speeds in a safe and fair manner, and moral questions about the point of continuing further down this rabbit hole when the average highway speed limit in the U.S. is 65 mph[7]. Regardless, the flood gates have opened. In the same 30-year span it took Porsche and Ferrari to best the record by 33 percent, Koenigsegg and Bugatti have overtaken them by a further 28 percent. (It's unlikely, but if that trend continues, cars will be capable of 355 mph by 2047.)

Even more striking may be the cumulative extent to which a variety of cars are able to replicate what the 959 and F40 did. Today there are 28 cars[8] that can hit 200 mph—including three American cars each priced under $100,000. In addition to their 200-mph mark, both the 959 and F40 were among the first production cars to accelerate from 0-60 mph in less than four seconds. In 2018 more than 40 cars can do it. And for increasingly cheaper prices. In 2004 the Ferrari F430 offered mind-melting acceleration with a 0-60 speed of just 3.9 seconds for the relatively affordable pricetag of $186,000. Four years later, the Nissan GT-R and its "video game" performance changed the game with a 3.2-second time for $70,000. And when the 707-horsepower Dodge Challenger SRT Hellcat came along in 2015 it could hit 3.6 seconds for $58,000.

To learn more about the way modern speed has warped the expectations of the next generation, I turned to Ed Kim, an automotive analyst with the research group AutoPacific. Kim spent his young adulthood in Los Angeles under the hood of a 1992 Honda Civic, in the early days of the L.A. import tuner scene that later inspired The Fast and the Furious, trying to squeeze out any fraction of horsepower out of his tiny 1.6-liter four-cylinder engine. He agreed that top-end performance in the world's exotic cars has not only progressed at an amazing clip, it's also dragged lower-end cars along for the ride.

"The standards for what fast is has certainly gone up," Kim said. "I remember when I was in high school and reading that the Ferrari Testarossa can do 0-60 in four-point-something, that was just like 'Holy crap! How is that even humanly possible?' And now you don't have to spend much money to get to 0-60 in four-point something. A Subaru WRX STi will get you there. A Ford Focus RS will get you there. Any number of cars under $40,000 will give you that sub-five second 0-60 time."

As more automakers started to figure out how to bring once-mega performance into their cars, they spread the technology across different models at different price points. And over time, they learned how to not only increase speed and capability but also how to effectively manage it. "An automatic-equipped Camaro ZL1, you could give to your grandmother to easily drive to the store and back," Kim said. "If you drive it like a car, it's just a car. To get that level of performance in the past you had to put up with a lot of sacrifices in drivability and ease of use—that's just not the case anymore. Nowadays I'll be very disappointed in a performance car if it makes me sacrifice drivability, comfort and a reasonable amount of refinement."

This is the environment pushing street-legal performance higher and higher. It's the environment that made the McLaren Senna possible, and created the technology that caused my body to float every time Gordon stabbed the accelerator pedal. The Senna is capable of a top speed of 208 mph. But you don't have to go that fast to have fun in a car. You don't have to buy a car with that kind of speed or a 3-second 0-to-60 time. It's all too easy to get fatigued with the onslaught of supercars rushing to an oversaturated market. Even Gordon and his fleet-owning friends acknowledged that the pinnacle of driving excitement is not speed in a straight line, but settling into a car with personality and character. And then wringing it for all it's worth.

There's an old saying in the car community that helps here. It's uttered at car shows across the country, printed in hundreds of articles each year and posted online every day. It's the antithesis of the horsepower wars. And it's fueling car culture today: "It's better to drive a slow car fast than a fast car slow."

Chapter II: The Absurdity of Speed

The original Ford Mustang launched in 1964 with a then-blistering 0-60 mph time of 8.2 seconds. Its abilities improved over time with some versions hovering in the 5-second range. Today, the slowest new Mustang does 0-60 mph in 5.2 seconds. A Mustang GT clocks 4.5 seconds. The upper echelon Mustang GT350R will pull to 60 in 3.9 seconds[9].

New cars are extremely fast. Advancements in engineering and technology progressed rapidly in recent years, to the point that even the slowest modern cars are capable of impressive performance. In the engine compartment new cars are equipped with direct injection, variable valve timing and turbocharging. Their frames are built of high-strength—and therefore low-weight—steel and composites. Their tires are grippy; their aerodynamics are slippery. They could slice through air like a sickle if they weren't barreling through it like a freight train.

In the 2018 model year, there are a number of cars that will do 0-60 mph in under three seconds. There are dozens that can hit 60 under four seconds. There are hundreds under five seconds.

But the most progress can be found in pedestrian cars. One study found that from 1976 to 2017 the average horsepower in U.S. passenger cars nearly doubled, from 145 to 283 hp. In that same time, the average zero-to-60 mph time of a typical new car was cut in half, from 14 seconds to just seven[10]. There is no better example than the quintessential family sedan. When Toyota launched its first Camry in the U.S. in 1983, the car had 92 horsepower and accelerated from 0-60 mph in 12.4 seconds. The all-new 2018 Camry has up to 301 horsepower. It reaches 60 mph in 5.8 seconds[11].

Do we really need all this speed? For decades the 0-60 mph time has been the hallmark of deciding whether a car is fast. Car fans debated in each others' basements for hours on end based on 0-60 acceleration times.

Magazines touted them on their covers. Car salesmen reeled them off with pride. But when blistering 0-60 times are so accessible—for $104,000 the Mercedes-AMG E63 S, a luxury sedan, will do it in 2.9 seconds—a change is in order.

Zero to 60 mph times are outdated as a concept. More to the point, they are not an accurate measurement of a car's overall capability and performance. Zero to 60 doesn't take into account attributes like braking, handling or balance. According to one test driver for a major manufacturer that I spoke with—who asked to remain anonymous in order to speak freely—it barely scratches the surface of automotive performance. "In the last probably 10-15 years mass market cars have gained so much performance that 0-60 is pretty much irrelevant," they said.

Modern cars use advanced technology to achieve levels of speed and performance that were once unthinkable. It's now easy to manufacture speed. What still eludes many automakers is the thing that drew most enthusiasts to the world of cars in the first place.

While you may be able to make a car scream from 0-60, it's many magnitudes harder to build a car with character. Does it talk to you? Does it dance? Does the car feel like an extension of your fingertips and toes? Does the car tell a story? Does the car make you *feel something*? These are the central questions that car enthusiasts ask themselves these days. Even with The Driver and his McLaren Senna, during lunch at a table filled with the car collector elite, the keepers of stables upon stables of ultra-performance cars, the phrase "Slow car fast" draws nods of affirmation. They want something emotional and rewarding and that maybe makes life a little bit difficult. Speed is a by-product. They want a love story.

*

As automakers wrest control away from those behind the wheel, enthusiasts are thirsting for ways to retain their grip on manual tasks. For example, the test driver I spoke with pointed to one vehicle that regularly puts a smile on the face of car fans: the Toyota 86. Built as a partnership between Toyota and Subaru, it's sold as the 86 and Subaru BRZ, an adorable and playful car offering buyers a hardtop alternative to the Mazda Miata. The unique thing about the 86/BRZ is that since its debut in 2012 it's been almost chronically underpowered. In seven years the 86/BRZ has never offered more than 205 horsepower from the factory. It's not very fast by modern standards and doesn't set any lap records. And yet the 86/BRZ makes people smile. It has rear-wheel-drive, a stiff chassis and offers a six-speed manual transmission. You sit low and get direct feedback from the heavy steering wheel. At $27,000 it's affordable, accessible fun. To many feeling suffocated by the horsepower wars, it's a breath of fresh air.

The allure of driving a slow car fast—that is, taking a car you might not traditionally think of for its speed and wringing every last bit of performance out of it like a sopping washrag—holds special appeal. In an age where we can measure a car's performance from top speed to 0-60 and G-forces, enthusiasts have gone in search of something that can't be quantified. In the world of sports this is called intangibles—the things that don't show up in a stat sheet but are still valuable and contribute to winning. Things like hustle. Things like vision, awareness and competitive spirit. While the automotive old guard is used to measuring horsepower and 0-60 times like home runs, touchdown passes and scoring average, the new school is looking for Wins Above Replacement for baseball, Defense-adjusted Value Over Average for football and Player Efficiency Rating for basketball.

"It can't be like the cars of yore with 300 horsepower that couldn't turn or stop," the test driver told me. "It's easy now to make 500-600 horsepower with turbos. But the cars have gotten big and heavy. All that mass requires more mass because now I need bigger tires, springs, sway bars. Mass begets mass, basically. Getting all that turned and flowed and making it live while you're doing it is getting harder and harder."

In sports, the advanced metrics create a more accurate portrait of a player's overall contribution to winning. In cars, it all adds up to engagement, a direct connection between man and machine. The sensation is amplified when you're pushing a car to its limits, which is more affordable and easier to achieve if you're driving a slow car, like a used BMW 3-Series or Ford Fiesta, fast. It's better than driving a fast car, like a modern Ferrari 488 or Nissan GT-R, slowly. It might be better than driving a fast car fast.

How do you more accurately determine overall performance? What's the automotive equivalent of Win Shares? Many would say it's lap times. To accelerate from zero to 60 mph a car must simply have an engine and four wheels. To competently make it around a racetrack, you have to take all the components and abilities of a car into account. If a car is fast but heavy it will need to brake earlier and lose valuable time. If a car has poor balance and handling it can't carry as much speed through the corners. If a car has bad aerodynamics it can't develop enough downforce and grip to make the best use of its tires.

If a car can do all of those things it will be capable of quick lap times—even in the absence of top horsepower and speed. Lap times are about measuring the overall balance and cohesiveness of a car. In many ways it has come to replace 0-60 as the most accurate way to quantify automotive performance. On the Internet competing fans threw out the lap times of their favorite car to assert its dominance. On the UK television program Top Gear, a cultural touchstone for millions of automotive enthusiasts around the world, the weekly rankings of cars' Power Lap times around its home test track became the definitive measuring stick for the fastest and most capable cars in the world.

Other tracks are also popular measuring sticks for performance. WeatherTech Raceway Laguna Seca and Virginia International Raceway are used regularly by automotive magazines to test cars' mettle against one another. And track records are falling all the time. During the 2018 edition of Car And Driver's annual test event at VIR, three different cars—the McLaren 720S, Chevrolet Corvette ZR1 and Porsche 911 GT2 RS—each set a new fastest lap ever recorded there[12].

But the undisputed king of putting cars to the test is the Nürburgring. The Nürburgring is a massive motorsports complex nestled deep within the overwhelming green forests of western Germany. Built in the 1920s, it has hosted thousands of major and international sporting events including

Formula One. There are several configurations ranging from the 3.2-mile circuit for Grand Prix races to the 16-mile combined track for special events. It's popular not only for sanctioned racing but also amateur drivers who pay a small fee to drive at their own pace, whether to hone their skills or just for the sheer thrill. The pavement dives and twists with hundreds of turns at challenging angles and speeds. It winds through the Eifel mountains and experiences a change in elevation of more than 1,000 feet. More than 200 people have died there. Three-time Formula One champion Jackie Stewart famously called it the "Green Hell."

When most people talk about the Nürburgring, they're really talking about the Nordschleife, or North Loop, the 12.9-mile section most commonly used by enthusiasts and manufacturers. It's a torture chamber for performance cars, with sections for top speed and hard braking and high-downforce cornering sometimes rolled into one. In the 1990s, auto manufacturers began to publicize the lap times their latest cars had achieved on the track, and interest grew in which cars could tackle the challenge of the Green Hell best. Today, Ring times are big business. Dozens of companies have established permanent homes around the track. More than 30 of them combined to form the Industry Pool[13], an organization that collectively uses resources to rent out the track for private testing.

Sometimes the automakers test at The Ring to ensure quality control, using the challenges of the track to highlight any weaknesses or structural improvements needed before a new model goes on sale. But often they are there to compete. A top lap time at the Ring can mean a flood of headlines and invaluable brand cachet. It was once thought impossible for a road-going car to break an 8-minute lap on the Ring. Today there are some lapping under 7 minutes. Porsche and Lamborghini in particular have traded blows in recent years for the top spot[14]. But now even sedans, station wagons and SUVs are competing for bragging rights there.

There's the Alfa Romeo Stelvio Quadrifoglio, a 505-horsepower crossover, set a new record for fastest SUV around the Ring in 2017, only to be topped by the Mercedes-AMG GLC63 S a year later[15] and then a Lamborghini Urus after that. Alfa again took a record for fastest sedan with its Giulia

Quadrifoglio, but it slipped away when the Porsche Panamera Turbo lapped faster. Six weeks later Alfa went back out with an automatic transmission and snatched it back[16]. The back-and-forth is enough to make your head spin. But it makes people take notice.

Backlash to Ring times is well underway. Some automakers have soured on the practice and a growing number of enthusiasts tend to downplay its importance as well. One supercar owner described it to me as "the ultimate useless dick-measuring contest." Testing for weaknesses is one thing, the argument goes, but developing and tuning a car specifically for one track doesn't necessarily translate to good performance everywhere. Or, for that matter, a positive ownership experience. Plenty of owners aren't going to drive their supercars quickly one single time, after all.

"If the goal is to understand how fundamentally capable a car can be in a variety of conditions, then the Ring is a great place for that," the test driver told me. "In order to be fast around the Ring a car has to be so good in so many areas that it is a reasonable measure of a car's maximum potential. But in my mind, we need a metric more focused on measuring the emotional response to an automobile. The measure shouldn't be on a closed course with professional drivers looking for maximum performance. It should be something more closely related to the manner the buyer will operate it. It should be from the perspective of a mere mortal. Because what that person will experience is much different from what a pro will experience. What's thrilling to me is to come off the corner and give it 40-50 percent throttle, and it's pulling hard, and makes the driver confident and makes them smile. I think that's a much more important metric than how fast it went around the Ring."

The Ring isn't a perfect measuring stick. But it has helped raise the bar for modern capability in normal cars. The lessons learned from hard testing resulted in incremental improvements that spread across automaker lineups, especially over the last decade. Cars have become lighter, more powerful, more agile and more efficient—simultaneously. They make more with what they have available.

With cars at all price levels starting with better bones that can handle more power and capability, automakers have leaned into taking normal models and sprouting performance versions out of them. That is, they take slow cars and turn them into very fast cars. Nowadays there is a performance version of nearly every vehicle on the market. There is the Volkswagen Golf "GTI" and the "R." There is the Hyundai Veloster "N." Cadillac has its V series and Alfa Romeo has its Quadrifoglio line. Infiniti has Red Sport models and Jaguar has an SVR house. There are Nissan NISMOs and Volvo Polestars. You can buy a Tesla in P100D trim. There is an AMG version of every Mercedes-Benz on sale. BMW has the M; Audi has the RS. There is even the Ford F-150 Raptor, a max-speed, high-performance pickup truck.

One of the hottest cars in enthusiast circles today is the Honda Civic Type R, a revived nameplate that reached near-mythic status because it was not available in the U.S. during its initial run from 1997-2017. Honda finally introduced a U.S.-spec Type R in 2017, offering Americans 300 horsepower and in a four-door hatchback for $35,000. It broke the front-wheel-drive Nürburgring lap record and still gets 28 mpg on the highway.

These were once slow cars that have now grown very, very fast. When it comes to new cars, the typical sedan idling at a stoplight is now capable of speeds once thought reserved for the Ferraris and Porsches of the world. In fact, compared to what our grandparents grew up driving, we're all inside rocket ships every day. And it's warped our perception of speed.

*

To find out more about how modern cars have become so fast and so powerful, I met with Eric Noble, co-founder and president of The CarLab, an automotive consulting firm. CarLab works with automakers to determine what new vehicles they should launch, what consumers are looking for and where automotive trends are headed. We met in his office, an open-floor computer warehouse in downtown Orange, Calif. with a storefront library filled from floor to ceiling with books on cars—the oldest was from 1907. In his four decades of working in the auto industry, one of the biggest changes Noble has seen is the steady march toward higher horsepower.

"Average speeds have gone up so much," Noble said from an armchair beneath the stack of books. "Today a Ford Fusion Sport would kick a Porsche 911 SC's ass."

Noble spends a lot of time studying what people buy and why. CarLab specializes in determining the trends in design, comfort, entertainment, engineering and pricing that help automakers make decisions about what they bring to market. What he's seen mirrors a wave of reports on typical U.S. buying habits. The thing that often motivates people isn't what you might think. It's rarely value, or brand loyalty or even quality. It's convenience. And more power under the hood gives you an advantage over others on the road.

"It's not because we're a bunch of hot-rodders," Noble said. "It's because it saves us time. We just get places quicker. Imagine that in 1976 the whole nation was driving 55 mph. Today that speed would be unacceptable at any level. Not because people are more performance-minded but because people just want to do things quicker. So the result has been cars that are just radically capable."

A child of the 1960s, Noble paints an interesting portrait of the progression of vehicle performance over the last several decades. He knows that 0-60 acceleration dominated the minds of car guys in his day, lusting for speed in the lead-up to an oil crisis. Then, subsequent power restrictions on engines in the '70s and '80s left most new cars listless and wanting.

"We were so starved for absolute performance that we'd take anything," Noble said.

He pointed to the 1976 Porsche Turbo, a car that marked a monumental leap forward in achieving performance under difficult circumstances. Looking back, he said, the '76 Turbo didn't offer much in the way of engagement and feedback. It suffered from difficult handling, poor throttle modulation and legendary turbo lag. But it didn't matter.

"It's collectible now but it wasn't that rewarding to drive," he said. "We wanted it so badly that the actual user experience wasn't even something we were worried about. All we knew was that thing would do 0-60 in 5.5 seconds and I think it did a top speed of 155. And that was it. The orthodontist had one and you wanted one."

Today, no one is starved for power. And that has led to enthusiasts that demand more from their cars, and value characteristics like feel and diversity of choice. In the same way that Millennials are more likely than other generations to ride fixed-gear bicycles, rehab vintage watches and buy heirloom tomatoes at farmer's markets, they are searching for something real and tangible in their cars. Noble believe it's a response to the ease and availability of speed.

"Gen Y values diversity in itself and in all things," he said. "It's manifest in their dress, it's manifest in their music. We have whole architectural conferences now that are devoted to surfaces, because it's what we tangibly interact with. Surface, feel and materials. We're just as physical and we get less physicality in our regular lives. We want to interact with things."

That may explain why one of the most advanced cars in recent history is also one of the most polarizing. When the Nissan GT-R debuted in 2008, it offered incredible performance at an paltry price. For less than $80,000 you could roll off the showroom floor in a four-seater sports car capable of 0-60 mph in less than three seconds. It laps the Ring in the realm of Porsches, McLarens and Ferraris. And it kind of feels like cheating.

Auto writers immediately lauded the GT-R for its fantastic speed but slammed its "video game" feel. The car was extremely advanced for its time, run by a multitude of sensors and internal control units that dictated how to best translate its formidable power to the road. Tasks that were once left to the skill and judgement of the driver were left to computers in the name of performance. It was fast as hell. Was it fun? A lot of people would say no.

Maybe the GT-R is the '76 Turbo of its day, Noble suggests. A car that achieved landmark performance but doesn't offer much in the way of feedback. The Porsche launched a revival of technological progress; the Nissan forced the hands of performance automakers to digitize and turbocharge their performance cars. Being smoked by an affordable Japanese brand was too much to handle.

"That car is the reason Ferraris are all-wheel drive now," Noble said. The GT-R showed that a group of enthusiasts prefer tangible driving to accessible speed. "That's why a Porsche 911 GT3, for instance, is far more embraced by the enthusiast community than the 911 Turbo. The Turbo is a faster car, but the GT3 is more affordable and more beloved. It requires more skill. It's less technologically advanced and more raw."

Noble isn't the only one who noticed that the fastest car isn't always the most desired. In early 2016, Porsche revealed the 911 R. The R designation paid homage to classic Porsche rally cars, but it may as well have stood for "Revelation." The 911 R was a version of the high-octane GT3 RS, but lighter, less flashy and more direct[17]. It had the same engine, but less weight. Unlike its GT3 RS sibling, the 911 R had no rear seats, no giant spoiler, no stereo and no air conditioning. Crucially the 911 R was only available with a six-speed manual transmission—a throwback since the GT3 and GT3 RS both were sold exclusively with automatics, and other versions of the 911 used a seven-speed manual. The goal wasn't to make the 911 R as fast as possible, or as quick around a racetrack. The goal was to provide the most direct, engaging and rewarding driving experience.

"All 911s are fast now, so I want a tactically rewarding experience," Noble said. "In fact if it's a little slower, I'm okay with that. If I can't shift as fast as the automatic gearbox, I'm okay with that."

Buyers were more than okay. The 911 R sold for about $180,000, but within weeks the demand pushed its value higher. Porsche made fewer than 1,000 and the used market flooded with low-mileage or no-mileage 911 Rs, with prices skyrocketing to $1 million[18].

Porsche had not anticipated this response, and it reacted accordingly. A year later it announced the GT3 Touring Package, a similarly bare bones GT3 with a six-speed manual that undercut the 911 R with a price at $143,000 and much more production capacity. This slashed 911 R prices—which solved a problem for Porsche as its customers flipped the cars as fast as they could—but it was also a recognition that the market could support a car that deliberately held performance back in the name of direct engagement.

*

"If you had a car that was as fast relative to the market but was unrewarding from an analog experience, it'd be received like the GT-R was—interesting but not demanded," Noble said. "I think that's the difference. Yeah, the GT3 is slower than the 911 Turbo—has anybody ever had to apologize for that? I don't think so. That goes right back to modern architecture, the passion for surfaces. We're focused on the tactile because we get less of it elsewhere."

While Noble talked I thought about the passionate people I've met in more than a year of cruising car shows and crashing people's garages. I thought about Dropped Alfa. I thought about the rewarding experience people get from driving very slow cars very fast. I thought about slow cars turned into fast cars like the Ford Focus RS and Honda Civic Type R. I thought about truly fast cars like the McLaren Senna, and how many different kinds of hypercars, supercars and fast cars in general there are these days. Making everything fast didn't kill our need for speed. It diversified it.

Cars have been gradually transforming from hand-operated machines into automatic ones "since the keterine self-starter," Noble said. "That was a manual task. We had cruise control introduced by Chrysler. That was automation. None of this is new. We generally want to have the task removed from us. But the focus will be more and more intense on the areas that remain, that we have to perform ourselves."

*

In early 2018 I met for coffee with Iliya and Nikita Bridan, identical twins who immigrated from Canada to the U.S. as teenagers to pursue their dream of becoming car designers. Today, Iliya works for Honda; Nikita for General

Motors. But what's special about the twins, at 31, is their passion project: a 1974 Alfa Romeo GTV 2000—bruised, dented and even rusted in some places—converted into a safari car. The Bridans had planned to race the Alfa. But en route to a shop for new parts the car fell off the back of a tow truck and smashed its rear end. To most people the next step may have been an expensive fix or a long-term space in the driveway. To the Bridans the next step was to bash it up some more. It became a rally car. It became known as "Dropped Alfa." And it's a car show celebrity.

The Bridans have taken Dropped Alfa desert drifting, rock-climbing and overlanding. To them the car has unlocked a new frontier of automotive thrills. It's also inspired a wave of fans to follow the same path. "That's probably the next big trend in car culture," Iliya told me. "I think that's why off-roading is about to explode. Modern cars are so lame you can only have fun out in the desert these days. All the canyons are policed, cars are so fast that if you push them in the canyon you're going to die if you crash. Back in the day you could go 40 mph and feel like it's fast. That's why we love old cars."

Within weeks of creating an Instagram account for Dropped Alfa, the twins had attracted thousands of followers. The car draws attention wherever it goes. Part of the appeal is that it's simply rare to see a GTV 2000, let alone one jacked up and dirty as all hell. Another part is, upon closer inspection, the insane level of detail that went into it. The Bridans custom built their own roof rack and chose overly aggressive ATV tires over more traditional all-terrains. Every bit of the car was poured over in three-dimensional CAD designs before they ever installed a part. The result is a meticulously designed vehicle that looks like it was thrown together overnight.

The first time I saw Dropped Alfa in person was at the Pelican Parts car show in Palos Verdes, an upscale peninsula south of Los Angeles. Pelican Parts is a small shop specializing in Porsche parts that has been hosting a bi-monthly event in its parking lot for years. Recently it's grown in size and star power. The day I went, a Saturday in early 2018, a Ford GT and a Porsche Carrera GT and two Singer Porsches were lined up alongside each other. I spotted in-the-know cult classics from the '80s like an Escort RS2000, a

Buick Grand National and a BMW Alpina station wagon. A Ferrari F40 filled up my rearview mirror as we coasted into the lot together.

Off in the corner, past dozens of 911s, up against the wall in a sparsely populated section of the lot, sat Dropped Alfa. It has an unmistakable grey and yellow paint scheme. Next to it sat two Mazda Miatas—both lifted, safari-style. One, called the Rallyata, wore grey and red and had two spare all-terrain tires mounted into a cutout section where its trunk used to be, like a trophy truck. The other had a red body with a white hood and the Mexican flag emblazoned across it. All three looked like the cheapest and least prestigious cars at the show. And all three looked like the most fun.

Even at a show packing millions of dollars worth of collectibles—with many capable of insane top speeds and some even with real racing pedigree—people began to gravitate toward the misfits. With their dented bodies, chopped fenders and brash colors, the three safari cars stood out in ways the other cars couldn't. They were dirty. They were rude. They had character. A handful of onlookers turned into a crowd. Soon the crowd turned into a mass of folks jostling to get a shot of all three in one frame. Pointing and chuckles turned into dropped jaws and excited squeals.

The brothers laughed as we recalled the story. They agreed that people are attracted to Dropped Alfa because it mixes a time when cars were more raw, less digital and more rewarding. The Bridans once owned a 2003 BMW M5 but couldn't stand it; it was too good. There were not enough imperfections to fix. Not enough room to play. So they stick to old cars. At the moment they drive the Alfa and a 1972 Porsche 911 in red-and-white Marlboro racing paint. They like looking at new cars, but can't bring themselves to find them interesting. When a neighbor brought home a new Porsche GT3—regarded widely as the perfect modern sports car—they couldn't help but imagine, unhappily, how easy it must be to get groceries with it.

"With old cars there's that romance," Nikita said. "You can be your hero. It's an era where if you wanted to go drive you had to tune the car up a little bit. It was like an experience."

"Slow car fast," Iliya said. "That's what we live by."

Chapter III: The Millennial Myth

As the American economy dragged itself out of the economic downturn in the early 2010s, analysts began to notice young people were delaying their driver's license test for months or even years. Some weren't bothering to get their license at all. One study from the University of Michigan Transportation Research Institute[19] found that driver's licenses among Millennials aged 20 to 24 dropped 16.4 percent compared with people the same age in 1983. For those 25 to 29 it dropped 11 percent. And for 30 to 35 it fell 10.3 percent. They also weren't buying new cars at the same rate of previous generations. It didn't take long for critics to make a diagnosis: Millennials hate cars.

Millennials are Americans born between the years of 1981 and 1996[20], which is to say, most adults. In 2020, that makes them between 24 and 39 years old. Millennials are now estimated to be the largest generation by population in the United States, numbering somewhere in the 73 million range[21].

With so much purchasing power, it's a big deal if all that consumer capital decides to simply up and stop buying cars. Evidence suggests that isn't what happened, however. National student loan debt grew by 102 percent from 2009 to 2019, according to Bloomberg[22]. Yet college is more of a necessity to a build a career than it has ever been before. So Millennials stayed in school longer and started having families later in life. Many of them, like myself, entered the job market in the midst of the Great Recession that caused the unemployment rate to double in just two years[23]. A 2018 study found that millennials make an average 20 percent less than baby boomers did at the same age, despite being better educated[24]. Millennials were playing against a stacked deck.

But media outlets didn't pick up on the causes, and their headlines grew dire:

"Why Young Americans Are Not Buying Cars," read *CNN Money*. "As Young Lose Interest in Cars…" began one story in the *New York Times*. *The Atlantic* especially took aim, running headlines such as "Why Don't Young Americans Buy Cars?" and "How Do You Sell a Car to a Millennial?" within two weeks of one another. Its coup de grâce crudely lumped millennials together as simply "The Cheapest Generation."

Millennials were blamed for the decline of everything from shopping malls and chain restaurants to soap. But cars seemed to be where most reporters focused their attention. In 2013, USA Today simply stated "Millennials Reject Car Culture."

Today, it's widely accepted that Millennials are flexing their buying power. "Millennials like buying cars after all," read CNBC in 2017. A report by the Specialty Equipment Manufacturers Association, or SEMA, found that young drivers aged 16 to 24 spent more than $7.2 billion on customizing their vehicles in 2017 alone. More than a third of the accessorizers in this age range said they love cars and most would rather give up their phone for a week than their car. "Young people age into driving and accessorizing," said the SEMA report. By the time of the report, Millennials had matured into an economic force. They had also begun to build rich relationships with cars, using social media to connect with one another and take car culture in new and exciting directions. Which made it all the more surprising when an automotive institution got it so wrong.

*

The November 2017 cover of *Car And Driver*, the 75-year old bible for generations of automotive enthusiasts, is shrouded in blackness. There is no photo of an Italian coupe screaming around a corner; no glamour shot of an American pony car dusting its tires into oblivion. There is only a black swatch, with the familiar *Car And Driver* header in bright white letters and a single question, in a slightly different shade of black, running down the right side of the page: "Driverless cars are supposedly imminent," it reads. "Is Driving Dead?"

It feels like an obituary. The cover could not be a further departure from that of a typical issue. It also represents a monumental shift from decades of tradition of breathlessly arguing for the value in driving excitement and passion. Outlets like these existed through the 1970s oil crisis, the 1990s plastic invasion and the 2008 economic apocalypse—all the while espousing the merits of enough horsepower to drag race a battleship across their pages. The "Is Driving Dead?" cover said that the end of all that is near. The end of what, exactly, is unclear. Horsepower? Speed? Overall performance? The very act of driving itself? Before I could read what the issue was arguing, I had a feeling I knew who was going to take the brunt of the blame.

For the special issue with a 31-page insert on the topic of driving's death, *Car And Driver* enlisted the help of journalist and author Malcolm Gladwell. Since Gladwell's debut in 2000 his five nonfiction books have collectively spent thousands of weeks on the New York Times Best Sellers list. A megastar of behavioral science and self-professed car guy, the mere appearance of Gladwell in the pages of *Car And Driver* promised a heftiness and finality to whatever argument he chose to make. When Gladwell writes, people listen.

To its credit, the staff of Car And Driver accomplishes the goal Alterman lays out in his opener. Within the special section there are dozens of articles[25], heavily sourced and researched, explaining complicated technical advances and examining their impact on the future of transportation. (Of particular excellence is Tom Vanderbilt's look[26] into the hurdles autonomous technology faces and at what point society agrees that pretty good autonomy is good enough.) The reader comes away more informed on the security, regulatory and economic challenges barreling toward society in an increasingly autonomous future. It's a thorough and level-headed analysis.

Where the issue falters, however, is with Gladwell. The guest editor authored two essays, ruminations on what the future holds for enthusiasts that bookend the special section. The first is titled "What happens when we give up control?" The second is called "Whither car culture?" They are both critical essays on the topic of modern car culture and what will happen to the automotive enthusiast in the midst of so much uncertainty. The problem is that they are important not because they are accurate portrayals or insightful predictions of the issue at hand but because they are exactly the wrong way to think about Millennial car guys.

Gladwell's first essay, the one about giving up control, portends to lay out the nature of the project and offer some clarity about its objectives. He observes that the age of autonomous driving is upon us, before we've really had a chance to sort out what that means and what it will look like.

There is a lot of truth in that statement. Automakers and technology companies are hurtling toward autonomous technology at breakneck speed, investing heavily in advanced safety features such as automatic emergency braking, adaptive cruise control and lane keep assist already in new cars on the showroom floor. Tesla's maligned Autopilot system is the posterchild for this integration, available on almost every model the company sells. These are technically all "automated" features, meaning the driver is controlling the car's speed, destination and other settings and allowing the machine to handle small tasks. But this is only the first step. Full autonomy in production vehicles is still the goal and we do have a lot to learn between now and then—we could all stand to learn more.

However Gladwell stumbles from there. He builds the crux of his argument on two source pieces: "The Chauffeur Problem" by Kevin Borg and "Have Smartphones Destroyed a Generation?" by Jean M. Twenge. He will use them to argue that Millennial apathy and disruption threatens to steal the joy of driving excitement from the grip of our driving gloves.

"The Chauffeur Problem" is a fascinating tale. Gladwell calls it an essay but it was actually Borg's doctoral thesis, written in 1999 during his Ph.D. candidacy at The John Hopkins University. In it, Borg details how the earliest car owners, wealthy aristocrats in the early 1900s, lived at the mercy of their chauffeurs. Owners relied on their chauffeurs to maintain and operate their vehicles because the engineering was too complicated to learn to do it themselves. Chauffeurs literally held the keys at all times and, basically, it turned into Chauffeurs Gone Wild. They loaned out their employers' cars for extra cash and terrorized neighborhoods with reckless joyrides for fun. Helpless, owners complained to anyone who would listen. Automotive publications overflowed with letters, and then produced in-house editorials advocating for stricter laws on chauffeurs (this is eventually how the driver's license was invented). It was a lesson, Gladwell writes, in the thorniness of adopting new technology and giving control of it to someone else.

This sets up the first half of the essay, followed by Twenge's article during the second half. Gladwell offers her piece up as evidence that vibrant car culture is disappearing as we know it. Twenge's point is that the ubiquitous nature of smartphones is making a generation of young people lazy, listless and depressed.

Few, in fact, had ever agreed on this point. Twenge's piece was widely panned by behavioral scientists after it was published by *The Atlantic* in 2017. It's true that young people are depressed and at risk of committing suicide at a higher rate than previous generations[27], according to the Center for Discovery, which provides mental health and substance abuse treatment. But the reasons are more nuanced than smartphones. Leading causes of depression today include increased pressure to succeed, financial worries and more access to alcohol and drugs. Twenge also ignored studies that show increased social media use can actually improve teenagers' intelligence, awareness and connection to one another, Cavanaugh wrote in Psychology Today.

Gladwell wrote on. Automobiles are about to enter an age of disruption akin to the arrival of smartphones a decade earlier, he said, and the same risks apply. His argument is that the apathy of teenagers toward car culture makes them susceptible to adopting whatever featureless, non-involving, self-driving vehicles are placed in front of them.

Here, Gladwell attempted to absolve auto manufacturers—the ones actually building and selling these cars—of their responsibility. He assures his readers that they are not the problem. And he conjures up the tired trope of horizontal teenagers who don't care enough about the thing you care about. The argument is that lazy teens will lead to a nation too preoccupied to drive itself. But there's not enough evidence to back it up.

The main problem with Gladwell's conclusion is that he never draws one. The essay never truly aims to answer its own question, which is, "What happens when we give up control of our cars?" Instead it warns of a vague and unnamed problem caused by lazy teenagers, but never explains what the problem is or how it will affect us.

If the article doesn't offer answers, what is its main takeaway? To many, the lasting impression will be the one Gladwell painted of young people sprawled onto the couch with a death-grip on their phone. It's relatable, easy to scapegoat and reaffirming a commonly-held fallacy. Under the structure of a weak sourcing and data, Gladwell has avoided answering difficult questions and appeased a frightened public. In the opening piece of a special edition.

Gladwell's other article is the outro, "Whither car culture?" Here, it would be extremely helpful to define car culture. Because car culture is not simply a mindset that is at risk of floating away. Car culture is a real and tangible thing that lives and breathes every day, in the form of car shows, car clubs, racing events and professional motorsports in every state. It is a unique social fabric comprised of long-lasting relationships between people and their shared connection through automobiles. To ask the question "Whither car culture?" is to plant the idea that an entire ecosystem of people and activities devoted to the invention that changed the social fabric of planet earth could disappear like soap suds down the sink. Gladwell points to recent shifts in the way we consume music, now almost entirely digital, as an example that the Internet era creates little emotional connection among listeners.

If anything, I would argue, music has taught us the exact opposite. The rise of digital streaming has fueled interest in a wider range of genres and artists than ever before, leading to the boom of festivals. More than 32 million people attended music festivals in the U.S. in 2014, according to Nielsen Music[28]. Nearly 15 million were Millennials. It does not seem feasible to argue that music has lost its "emotional intensity" unless you've never heard of Lollapalooza, Outside Lands, Burning Man and Coachella.

Cars are no different. Social media and the Internet have dumped kerosene on the campfire of automotive enthusiasm. Car lovers are not lying on the floor reading magazines while spinning vinyl, but they are scrolling Instagram to find local car shows while pumping Post Malone through their iPhones. Car shows are seeing higher attendance and greater frequency. Amateur motorsports have created new classes to accommodate a wider range of entries. Automotive festivals like Gridlife have followed the path laid before them by music festivals. Young people have not turned their backs on music and cars—they have turned them into fully-immersive experiences.

The problem here is that this is supposed to be about the death of car culture, not the worries of auto executives. In an article that purported to address the decline of car culture Gladwell asks us to consider the risk to earnings reports and quarterly profits. What does selling more Honda CR-Vs and Ford Fusions every month have to do with car clubs, weekend gatherings and group drives down the coast? The articles would have reflected that, if the writer had ditched the spreadsheets and gone outside to experience car culture—like Millennials are doing.

In a rare special edition of an automotive institution that aims to grapple intelligently with the ways technology will change society, Gladwell's two essays argue that young people like smartphones too much and that digital music proves we will lose our emotional connection to cars. His sources are heavily anecdotal, thoroughly contested, or his own father. He presents assumptions that are written as fact. But it lacks an awareness of the real changes going on outside.

The truth is that car culture is deep into a renaissance, fueled by everything they said would kill it, expanding into innovative avenues and reaching wider audiences that were unthinkable until recently. Often this growth is fueled by the very smartphones and young people that Gladwell—and by proxy *Car And Driver*—spent a lot of ink railing against. The reality is that car culture is more rich, mature, knowledgeable and perhaps most importantly, diverse than ever before. In an era where automotive content is lusted after with more ways to get it than ever before, *Car And Driver* opted to ignore and separate itself from the conversation. It looked down and scoffed. Or didn't look at all.

It's true that Millennials were slow to buy new cars. But the tables are turning. In California, Millennials in 2015 bought more cars than baby boomers for the first time. "Millennials like buying cars after all," declared CNBC. Even the declining driver's license phenomenon seems to have been overblown. The Transportation Research Institute at the University of Michigan found that U.S. citizens of all ages are turning away from licenses[29]. The trend wasn't an example of teenage laziness. It was a massive, intergenerational shift.

Millennials and post-Millennials are having deep and rewarding relationships with cars. Today's enthusiasts are from different backgrounds. They celebrate different types of vehicles and drive them in different ways. The age of the "car guy" bringing to mind a skinny white teenager in suspenders and a t-shirt under the hood of a '57 Chevy is over. Car culture is not dying—it's changing. The problem is that to people like Gladwell, that's the same thing.

Chapter IV: Checkered Flag

The first time I attended the Toyota Grand Prix of Long Beach I committed a crime. It was 2006, my junior year of college, and my first as a sportswriter for CSU Long Beach's student alternative weekly. As far as my editor and I could tell, our paper had never covered the race, just four miles from campus, in its 30-year history. In fact, I was shocked to learn the race existed, right in my backyard for the last 11 years. I had never heard about it.

I applied for a media credential and began to plan my attack on one of the most important street races in the world. The open-wheel racers of Champ Car took the main stage with big names like Paul Tracy, Jimmy Vasser and Sébastien Bourdais. Up and comers included Will Power, A. J. Allmendinger, Justin Wilson and Oriol Servia. The support series that weekend included the GT cars of Speed World Challenge and the prototypes of the Grand American Rolex Series[30], both now defunct. There was a lot to consider. So when my credential application came back with a denial, I knew it wasn't the end of my weekend.

Without a job at the time and not enough money for a date, let alone a race weekend, I improvised. I drove my '88 Fox-body Mustang GT into downtown Long Beach, found free parking in the sketchy lot of an abandoned building that's since been torn down for condos, and walked to the track. Stuffed into tight streets along the waterfront, at 1.968 miles a lap it's one of the shortest circuits that professionals will race all year. But the urban scenery is stunning.

The front straight pulls a long right-hand down Shoreline Drive up against the boardwalk and marina beside it. Racers swoop around a picturesque fountain of twirling dolphins, then blast through narrow passages with Art Deco era architecture looming overhead. The Queen Mary is easily visible in the background. The skies are always a stunning blue—it has rained on this weekend exactly once in 45 years. The race has earned nicknames like

"Monaco of the West." Drivers routinely call Long Beach the jewel of the Indycar schedule, right behind the Indianapolis 500 in terms of prestige.

I climbed up seven flights of stairs to reach the top level of a massive parking garage. The garage fills up fast on race weekend because the track runs right up against it. From any of the floors you could look down onto Turn 5, as the cars wiggled into a bumpy slow right and thundered up the road, passing under a massive bridge topped by a decorative roller coaster. The ocean was not far in the distance. You could hear the roar of the crowd and feel the pounding engines reverberate over the concrete and up into your throat. I stayed there for a few hours before feeling the urge to get closer.

I headed down to the street level and walked along the fencing hoping for a better look at the action. I won't go into details, but I found a way inside. Before long I was on track grounds. I'm not proud of sneaking into an event that holds a very dear place in my heart, but I felt pulled toward the track. Watching the cars, roaring down the same streets I drove all the time to go to the movies, was intoxicating. The crowd was enthralled and ready to party. It was a dream. I wrote a letter to the Grand Prix in my column that week, apologizing for sneaking in, but I also don't regret it. (Don't get any ideas. I've checked my point of entry many times and it's no longer possible.)

Ever since that year the Toyota Grand Prix of Long Beach has been a hallmark event for me, circled on the calendar long in advance. Lots of other people feel the same way. The 2018 event drew more than 185,000 attendees over the three-day weekend, according to organizers—the highest total since 2000[31]. I've always taken note of the high number of families, women and children in attendance, which stands out compared with most other motorsports events I've been to. Spend any time at the race and it's easy to believe that it has something to do with the event setup.

Not only is the Grand Prix set an urban waterfront in sunny Southern California, there's also a lot to enjoy besides the racing. The convention center has vendors and a kids' carnival. Outside, downwind of the grillers boasting foot-long hot dogs and turkey legs, there is an exotic car paddock, the garages for the IMSA WeatherTech SportsCar Championship are open and there are concerts when the sun goes down. The boardwalk restaurants lie within the track grounds and remain open through the weekend. The Grand Prix of Long Beach must be the only racetrack in the world with a Hooters within its confines.

During the 2018 running I spent hours walking the grounds—with an approved media pass, this time—just to chat with industry friends and scope out the scene. Outside the convention center, a radio station pumped country music to couples square dancing as IndyCars screamed around them. On the grassy walk between grandstands, a woman rode piggyback on her boyfriend and stole swigs out of the beer helmet on his head. Standing at the base of a giant rock-climbing wall, a young fan, maybe 8 or 9, peeked through his bangs and showed off the front fender of a Porsche 911 that had been ripped off during practice for the World Pirelli Challenge Series. The boy had passed by the Pfaff Motorsports garage at the right time and the team let him keep the fender. Driver Scott Hargrove autographed it[32]. Now the boy wouldn't let it out of his sight. He carried it halfway around the outside of the circuit and took it home as a souvenir.

*

The morning of the day before the main IndyCar race, I settled into one of my favorite viewing spots, a balcony overlooking Turns 2 and 3 that loop around the dolphin statue, to watch the drivers practice. The view is framed by palm trees. Racing at Long Beach has its drawbacks compared with a traditional race course. Street tracks are bumpy, the tight confines make for strained viewing and with little room for passing the race runs the risk of turning into a parade. But even on its worst day, there might not be a more beautiful place to watch racing.

I basked in the sun as the cars dove past the fountain until I felt the need to see them up close. I passed two teenagers snapping away with telephoto lenses, crossed the bridge over the track and leaned up against the fence on the other side. From here you can feel the cars come out of Turn 1 and lean on the power to pull them through a 90-degree left. This is on the other side of the faux-rollercoaster bridge, and from the ground, it looms high over the cars for a Coney Island effect.

Before long, practice was up. IMSA was up next and I wanted to find a grandstand seat to watch the thundering Corvettes and screaming Ferraris. I turned to find the boardwalk and almost bumped into the two teens again. Stringy and long-limbed, they'd been stalking the outside fence seeking any clean shot. One wore a Ford Motorsports hat, the other a Fontana Auto Club t-shirt and IndyCar hat. When they turned to leave, I stopped them. Jared Caylor and Noah Benton, both 17, were from nearby Palos Verdes. They'd driven over to Long Beach together to see the weekend's cars up close and hopefully catch a lucky shot.

I asked which motorsport they most enjoyed watching or shooting. "Whatever drives by," Caylor said. "Yeah, all the way up through the Super Trucks," Benton said. Both belonged to a car club at school, consisting of gearhead friends who cruised together and worked on their cars. Caylor even competes locally[33] in senior karting. On a beautiful Saturday in Southern California they had grins plastered across their faces. It was even Coachella weekend. These two teens passed on Beyoncé for BMWs.

I left them to their photos and headed to the IMSA garages. The longer I watch racing the more I become interested in the inherent connection shared between racing sports cars and the production cars they're based on. There's no better demonstration of that at the highest level than IMSA. Its sports car class consists of models resembling the Ferraris, Corvettes and Porsches in dealerships. There are also Cadillacs, BMWs, Audis and Acuras. Even when done up in racing livery and aero bits, there is still enough resemblance that casual fans can tell which car is which with a passing glance. And unlike the "stock cars" in NASCAR, these cars still use proprietary parts from their production cousins that separate one another from the rest of the field.

IMSA also has a class of prototypes, low-slung focused racecars with a single seat in the middle and bodywork that looks like it could fly through space. These are not based on production cars. They're much more akin to the world-beaters that compete in the 24 Hours of Le Mans and other endurance events. However there are still passenger car influences to be found. And in the field at Long Beach, none of the cars were a better representation than the Mazda DPi.

"This is a similar engine to the production cars," said Mo Murray, head of integrated motorsports marketing at Mazda, "but it makes about 600 horsepower." Murray conducted an overview of the car, pointing to each section as mechanics worked on every bolt and wire in a frenzy behind him. The car had just come in from a practice session and the team scrambled to download its data in preparation for the next round. As he spoke the occasional air gun would drown out his voice, or a mechanic would lift the entire front end to be repaired, or the shrieking motor would be started to check the cylinder firing pattern.

The Mazda DPi looks nothing like the Mazda next to you in traffic. Its brilliant candy red paint coats a very low and very long body. The fenders are cut out at the top to expose massive slick tires pushed out to the edges. A vertical fin rises from the top of the roof and extends all the way back to a rear wing the size of a park bench. The doors swing up like the wings of a beetle. The brakes cost $51,000. Each.

But the motor, the heart and soul of this banshee of a vehicle, is similar to one you can find on the road. It's a 2.0-liter four-cylinder, the smallest in the entire IMSA prototype field and the only four-cylinder. The engine is based on the MZR, a commonly used motor that Mazda has built and put into production cars from the MX-5 Miata sports car to the Mazda6 sedan. In the DPi, the engine has been turbocharged and pressurized within an inch of its life. Because of its small size, the engine produces more than twice the horsepower per liter of its competitors. It also uses less fuel and can stay on the track longer. Not bad for a motor commonly found in high school parking lots.

Murray rounded up Tristan Nuñez, a factory driver in the Mazda program. Statuesque with a bronze tan and the perfect coif of hair that only racecar drivers seem able to obtain, Nuñez was practically born to drive fast. He first got into karting as a 13-year-old growing up in Florida. His father is a tennis coach and began working with the son of Derek Bell, the decorated racing driver. When Nuñez's father told Bell his son was interested in motorsports, Bell's eyes lit up.

"He said, 'Heck yeah, let's get him in a go-kart and go to Homestead,'" Nuñez told me. Three years later, at 16, he signed to Mazda as a full-time driver and became the youngest to win his class in the series.

Now 22, Nuñez is seasoned to the ways of prototype racing. It's a high-stakes style of motorsport defined by millimeters and milliseconds, where speed comes easy and precision is what separates a great driver from a merely good one. These are not the hard-charging, hard-partying race days of yore. Prototype racecars, as with IndyCars and even GT cars, are capable of speeds and grip that enact punishing forces on drivers. For a car like the Mazda DPi, which has an improved suspension, more mechanical grip, more power and about 100 pounds less weight than its 2017 predecessor, its abilities are improving at a rate that is faster than the human body can handle. Around the most intense corners, such as "the kink" at Road America in Lake Elkhart, Wisconsin, the car corners at 4.5G without coming close to its limit.

For a driver like Nuñez, who has to endure that and myriad other high-G turns dozens and dozens of times in a single race, preparation is key. At 22, he is nearing the peak age for a racecar driver at this level. Because the cars are much more reliable, breaking the car is less of a possibility, and drivers are encouraged to push. Endurance races that once required the balance of speed and saving the car are now all-out sprints for up to 24 hours. Nuñez has learned some tricks. To take a corner like the kink at the rate he needs to stay competitive, he must suck in a deep breath before the turn, hold it, like a fighter jet pilot, and then let it out upon exit. Otherwise, the sheer force from the harness could bruise his chest or crack his ribs. "It sucks, I'm not gonna lie," he told me.

Already, his body takes more time to repair itself after a race than it did when Nuñez was a teenager. Drivers famously used to "train" by closing down the bar. Now, out of necessity, nutrition and fitness in motorsports has caught up to the rest of professional athlete standards. Nuñez stands 6'1", tall for a race driver—he calls himself "a monster"—and weighs 159 lean and chiseled pounds. He watches what he eats and combines weights with cardio in his workouts to train like an endurance athlete. If either his strength or his stamina diminish, driving a featherweight racecar with 600 horsepower suddenly becomes very difficult.

"The steering wheel's heavy, the brake pedal's heavy, you don't get the conveniences of a regular road car," he said. "If one guy's putting in as much effort as he possibly can physically he's obviously going to surpass everyone in his sport. Look at golfers now. That's where racing is too."

"The day after a race it's more than aches and pains," he said. "Your body is completely done, it's wiped. It's hard to get out of bed for a couple days. With long ones, like the 24 Hours of Daytona, you're feeling crappy for the whole week. My lower back and shoulders were killing me. When you're pushing the car to its limit it's a whole other story. Every second you gain in a race car feels physically worse. No matter how hard you work out your neck it's gonna be sore. The Gs you're pulling and you've got that heavy ass helmet on. Honestly everything hurts."

As much as that sounds like a nightmare, Nuñez happily puts in the time to make it possible. His training goes like this: in the offseason, two 90-minute workouts for a total of three hours a day; during the season, an hour per day of circuit training to hit all the muscle areas at once without straining anything too hard. His main focus is arms and legs to operate the car, core for stamina over the course of the race and neck to keep the weight of his helmet from tipping his head over. Low weight, high reps. Leading up to race day Nuñez does yoga to stay flexible and loose. His girlfriend is an instructor, which helps.

To feed the machine his diet is mainly chicken or fish, with a lot of greens and other vegetables. On race weekends the team provides a chef, but otherwise it's up to Nuñez to avoid sweets. Especially chocolate, his weakness. He practically giggles recalling a late-night run to McDonald's following the 12 Hours of Sebring, a rare treat after being tossed around the notoriously dilapidated airfield.

"A cheat meal after the race is fine," he said. "But we're very strict with ourselves."

*

Getting the most out of a driver means being kind to their bodies, too. Nowadays drivers rarely put in practice time on the track to hone their skills. It's too physically demanding. Instead, teams are turning to driving simulators not unlike the video games that millions of people play across the globe. For a group like the Mazda prototype effort, that means the Driving-in-Loop simulator, or DIL.

Built by MultiMatic, which also builds the driver containment tubs in the actual cars, the DIL consists of a real racecar setup in front of a huge cylindrical screen. It stands 1.5 meters tall and 4 meters wide, with 160 degrees of vision. The tracks are replicated down to each bump and crack in the road, which translate into the driver's seat thanks to feedback that turns pixels into realistic pitching and heaving around the circuit. The facility, known as the MultiMatic Technical Centre, resides in Ontario, Canada. Mazda prefers to send its drivers and engineers there to collect data and prepare for a race rather than risk harm to its cars and drivers on a real track. They typically spend two full days on the DIL before a race.

"It's the best way for a driver and engineer to get acquainted," Nuñez said. "You can constantly make changes on the fly, the engineers can explain changes and vice versa." But the experience is much more than just team-building and finding the braking zone. The car can be adjusted in the game just as it would in the real world. In the lead-up to Long Beach, two of Nuñez's teammates had never driven the course before, so they did 100 laps each on the simulator to prepare. The results have very real effects on race decisions. "If it works on the sim then we'll start with it on the weekend."

At Long Beach, Nuñez qualified the No. 77 car in seventh place out of 14. The driver who qualifies is required to start the race before handing off to a teammate for the finish. Nuñez started and stole a position before the mandatory driver switch with Oliver Jarvis to bring the No. 77 home. Up front the leaders shuffled around in a thrilling battle. All three top finishers took podium spots despite beginning the race outside the top three positions. From a seat in the grandstands, above the beginning of the front straightaway, I watched Jarvis jump up into a fourth-place finish just six seconds behind the winner. Nuñez and Jarvis finished ahead of their Mazda teammates in ninth place. They also took home valuable championship points for the season and even scored a faster single lap, a 1:14.297, than any of the three cars that finished ahead.

*

I was glad to see the Mazda team succeed. More than that I was thrilled to see such a huge variety of motorsports on display. After the IMSA race came Stadium Super Trucks, a mix between sports car racing and monster trucks with carnage, three-wheel cornering and jumps—yes, jumps—that launch the steroidal pickups 20 feet up into the air. IMSA gave race fans what they wanted. SST whipped the crowd into a frenzy.

Drifting followed. Long Beach is a special place for Formula Drift, the professional drift series going on its 15th season. Its office headquarters used to be right down the street and is now located in the Long Beach enclave of Signal Hill. Formula Drift typically holds a competition for championship points one week prior to the Grand Prix, taking over the weekend and descending upon the city with a fury of loud pipes and tire smoke, followed by a demonstration event during race weekend. For 2018, FD held its points event during race weekend. As the sun began to set and the day drew to a close, the grandstands along Turns 9, 10 and 11 swelled with fans. They were in for a show.

From my seat, two cars at a time came screaming into view to the left. They were fully sideways on a right-hander that immediately transitioned to a long, sweeping turn swinging from left to right in front of me. Now they're off to the right, tip-toeing into a hairpin right still tucked up alongside one another until they hammer out and run out of view. Smoke left in their wake filled up my entire field of vision as my adrenaline lingered. It's a challenging set of corners with no down time. Formula D drivers take the whole thing near triple-digit speeds. The sound and fury was unlike anything else that had been around the track that day.

On the first night of drifting, I was taken aback by the energy in the crowd. The drivers lined up to greet and wave to thundering applause. They then did tandem donuts, three groups at a time, some breaking off for their own theatrics, the crowd losing its mind. You could only see the spinning headlights through the smoke. Fans hanging from the balconies on high-rise condominiums could be heard screaming down onto the mayhem. It was still broad daylight. The competition hadn't started yet.

Polish driver Piotr Wiecek took home first place that night in a red, white and blue Nissan Silvia S15. It's not much different from the ones amateurs race around the world every weekend. It just has about 1,000 horsepower. Wiecek was impressive and made few mistakes, if any. But I found myself emotionally moved by the performance of American driver Forrest Wang, in a bright green S15, who positively danced on the tarmac. Each twist was a pirouette, each toss of the tail carried so much panache I didn't realize I was jumping up and down on the metal bleachers until the end of his run. Wiecek deserved the win. But Wang sold me on drifting.

On the second night, I considered myself an expert drifting judge. Once again Wiecek was impressive. Once again, in my amateur opinion, Wang was transcendent. His drifts were held longer, his tail came out farther. He put more pressure on the leader and he dared others to do the same with him in front. He made more mistakes, but when he's on it's like nothing I've seen in motorsport.

As the night rolled on, vendors strolled up and down the rows yelling "Cold lemonade!" and "Hot churros!" No clouds appeared in the crisp orange sky that casted a rose gold hue over everyone and everything at the track. I switched to the seats at the end of the hairpin, where you could catch the cars running through the sweeper at a distance and watch them come onto the straight up close. From here the view is punctuated by palm trees. The smoke drifts carried south to Orange County and combined to create a rubbery haze with the pinks and oranges of the horizon balancing atop the Pacific. There's nothing like racing in Long Beach.

A mother and father and their adult children were drunk to my right. The teenage girls to my left discussed drifting technique and whooped it up after every run. We all watched as the cars fly through the hairpin and come to a complete stop while they await scores from the judges. Smoke billowed out of the wheelwells and into the cabin for several minutes after each run ends. In the battle before the championship round, Wiecek and Wang were perfectly matched. Neither missed an inch. The judges decided two runs were not enough to choose a winner and they ran it back for a third time. This time, Wiecek barely edged Wang out to advance. He then defeated the Ford Mustang of Justin "JTP" Pawlak to claim his second win in two nights[34].

I was awestruck. The level of driving skill was certainly on par with anything I saw from IMSA or IndyCar drivers all weekend. But mostly at the fans, who packed the stands well into the dark of night. The enthusiasm never waned. They were just as hyped when Wiecek accepted his trophy as when the fun began. A standing ovation accompanied all the drivers who rolled out at the end of the show, many fans whistling and clapping with their hands held high. Pumping their fists. This is what love looks like. This is what passion and knowledge of the sport and appreciation of the skill looks like. All ages, all races. This does not look like a desperate industry or a struggling sport. I left with throngs of satiated fans. If car culture ever does truly die, drifting will be the last thing to go.

*

A few weeks later, I catch up with Nuñez. After the success at Long Beach he and the team tasted even more during the Acura Sports Car Challenge at Mid-Ohio, where they started and finished third[35]. After a rough 2017 season and a promising 2018 campaign Nuñez and Mazda finally captured the podium they had been close enough to taste. With a 10-second gap and a couple of laps to go, the team told Nuñez to relax and bring the car home. I asked what went through his mind in that moment.

"I disconnected from everything and focused on how the car felt. And it sounds stupid but I just became one with the car. We call that being in the zone. Your brain disconnects and it's doing it so naturally, you're hitting your perfect line every time. It's something I think every driver yearns for."

Here, Nuñez sounded like a different person than the one that earlier complained about the aches and pains, the workouts and the diet. The one who made the physical strain of racing sound like a sentence levied against him. I had started to wonder if the modern demands of racing made it possible to enjoy the simple act of driving.

Can you see yourself doing this the rest of your life? I asked.

"I still love getting up in the morning and going to the track," he said. "I'll do it until I'm not fast anymore."

Chapter V: How to Find the Car Guys

The whole world knows Detroit as the Motor City. That blue-collar town on the river is where cars as we know them today were shaped in molten steel and pounded into submission along the assembly lines. Detroit might be the birthplace and remains the hometown of the automotive industry; but Southern California is ground zero for car culture. Its arid climate, palm-tree-lined ocean roads and eccentric flair have inspired generations of auto enthusiasts.

The hot rod got its start here, when bored teenagers in San Pedro took their fathers' sedans to dusty shops and dropped in the biggest engines they could find. The concept of the convertible, the surf van and the beach Jeep all came from here. Black and Latino culture in East L.A. birthed the lowrider[36]; Asian-Americans in Gardena[37] introduced the import scene and drift culture to the U.S.[38][39] George Barris' Batmobile and Drag-U-La, followed by Greased Lightning, the DeLorean and The Fast & The Furious turned cars into big screen stars.

Wipe away the glitz and glamour, though, and L.A. people just love to drive. Some of the most scenic and twisty roads in the country can be found here, whether it's a sun-soaked jaunt up Pacific Coast Highway or a dive-bombing run through the canyons with stunning twists and turns. There are dry lake beds with no speed limits and off-road courses with no restrictions. There is a litany of racetracks for proving your mettle.

Speed shops have always thrived here. The quintessential example is So-Cal Speed Shop, a Burbank hot-rodding shop opened in 1946 by a released Air Force engineer named Alex Xydias. Using the belly tanker from a P-38 Lightning fighter plane, Xydias crafted a streamlined racer that combined striking post-war design and L.A. hot rod culture. The teardrop-shaped car took one high-speed record after another at the Bonneville Salt Flats, an expansive dry lake bed in the Utah desert. Southern California became the epicenter of speed. That hasn't changed a bit.

*

Just south of Los Angeles in Orange County, not far from where the Derelicts first mixed cars and coffee, the town of Newport Beach houses an unassuming industrial park with one unmarked glass door after another. Just before 7:00 a.m. on a hazy Saturday, the ocean salt hanging thick in the air, Joey Seely pulls into the parking lot and opens his shop.

Seely, 39, is the owner of E-motion Engineering, a garage that has earned a reputation for taking highly-capable sports cars and sharpening them into samurai swords of performance. The bulk of the work is on Porsche 911s, everything from the 930 era of 1980 to 87 that are crafted for cruising in car rallies to ferocious late models like the GT3RS, released in 2018.

He pulls into the lot in a teal 1966 Ford F-250 Camper Special with a "For Sale" sign in the windshield. Seely hops out wearing jeans and a t-shirt. He has sharp features, his nose and chin pointed at dramatic angles smoothed out by light stubble, and the rest of his face is hidden behind sunglasses and a Quiksilver hat. Seely looks more likely to cover *Surfer* magazine than climb under the fastest sports cars at the track. He slams the metal door on the pickup and pats the hood.

"Growing up I never had an appreciation for the old trucks," he says. "But now I do. I really like this thing."

With classic SoCal surfer looks and a dry sense of humor, Seely is dripping with character, which is fitting since customers come to E-motion because he knows how to bring out a car's personality. The trick of the Porsche 911 is that its engine is in the rear, giving it unique driving dynamics and a near-perfect 50:50 weight distribution from front to back. The better the balance, the more naturally the car will handle. Working his magic on the suspension settings, Seely understands how to highlight the car's natural characteristics.

He also installs new technology to deliver a better driving experience than even Porsche engineers envisioned.

"It's like *The Matrix*," Seely says. "I start changing components and moving it around in my mind." It's a unique talent. When clients bring their cars to E-motion, they are investing in Seely just as much as they are in a new car. More than one customer calls Seely a master of handling. "I just understand dynamics," he says.

Seely is originally from from New Hampshire. Growing up with a single mom, Seely and his older brother were not wrenching on cars as kids. Instead, they poured themselves into automotive magazines, dreaming of owning and racing European sports cars. At 20 he moved from his childhood home in New Hampshire to San Diego to chase that dream. He built club race cars for gentleman racers, then moved to Seattle to work on professional racing series. That led to a job in the American Le Mans Series, or ALMS, a now-defunct league featuring race-prepped sports cars like Porsches and Corvettes alongside prototype missiles with few rules and looked like spaceships. It was there, slogging away in cramped quarters for the Peterson Motorsports and White Lightning Racing team, that Seely developed his talent for finding the perfect balance of speed and handling in a car. In a highly competitive field teeming with fearless drivers, including a young Patrick Long in his first pro seat, Seely's cars won. A lot.

"We were one of two teams to beat Porsche with their own car," Seely says. The first was Joest, the storied outfit from Germany known for its stature in endurance racing. In 1992 the team privately entered a Porsche 962 in the 24 Hours of Le Mans and raced it against Porsche's own sponsored team. Joest took home the trophy. Years later the team was tabbed to run Audi's program at Le Mans and would claim nine first-place finishes in the world's most prestigious race, including three separate three-peats[40]. Nobody had beaten Porsche with their own car before, except Joest.

The win solidified the feeling inside Seely that his modifications were on the right track. Today, he makes Porsches better than Porsche does. Soon Seely's grin grows into a full-on smile as he recalls the victory that foreshadowed his second career.

After four years of racing in ALMS it was time to move on. Seely co-founded BBi Autosport, a performance garage in Huntington Beach for sports car clientele. With a racing heritage and no shortage of Porsche owners looking for bragging rights on their weekend cruises, BBi blew up. The staff quickly grew to 12 full-time employees. Orders piled high and deadlines became strict as cars needed to be finished to make way for the next client. Seely's partners wanted to expand beyond Porsche which would have increased the load even further. It weighed on him.

"Quality was sacrificed and the whole fun was sacrificed," Seely says. "The whole point of this is fun."

Seely stuck it out with BBi for eight years. In 2015 his partners bought out his share, and Seely used the money to start E-motion Engineering less than a mile away. It's quiet compared to the bustling BBi world he left behind. The only other employees are Devin, his assistant, and his brother, who runs operations. It takes time and money, but Seely does nearly all of the mechanic work himself.

"I wanted a very chill approach," he says. Business has been strong, with many of his old clients following Seely to the new shop, but it's a pace that he gets to dictate. "I do this because I love it and fortunately I've been able to make a living from it. I get to focus on big projects and keep on it."

One of the big projects he's undertaken at E-motion is known as Luft 001, an impeccable lifted 911 built by Seely, Long, fellow racer Jeff Zwart and a team of friends. The group auctioned off Luft 001 in 2016 to benefit pancreatic cancer research. A year later Luft 002 debuted with skid plates, mud flaps, metal bumpers and a rooftop rack in screaming "Signal Yellow" paint[41]. Luft 002 took the Safari 911 trend and stretches it to the limits. The engine, transmission and suspension were all reworked so that it became the exclamation point of Safari cars. It's also an awe-inspiring example of Seely's penchant for juicing Porsches for all they're worth.

Another pet project is a car lovingly named Project Nasty. A bright red assault on the senses, Project Nasty began life as a 1985 Porsche Carrera. As soon as Seely got it in 2007, he set to work making it unique. He drastically reduced the weight, nearly doubled the horsepower in the engine and dialed-in the suspension to his exacting demands. It has no windows and no interior. Project Nasty is Seely set between four wheels—and it was our ride for the day.

Getting into Project Nasty is an experience. The passenger side door is extremely lightweight. It swings out wide at the touch of a finger like it's been pent up for centuries, a genie waiting to be released. You lift your left leg over the door sill and plop down into the bucket seat made by renowned seat maker Recaro—"The lightest one they make," Seely says. The bottom of the seat curls up around your hips and squeezes like jeans three sizes too small. "They do need to make different sizes," Seely admits.

The tight seat, however, will soon come in handy. Project Nasty pulls out of the E-motion parking lot and cruises through lazy Huntington Beach as Seely recalls his racing days. The engine, behind us, purrs. Without windows to soundproof the cabin, each gentle application to the throttle can be felt through your whole body. It's a rattle, growing shriller by the second and underscored by a faint whine from the turbocharger, followed faithfully by a rumbling that brings a soothing substance to the experience. The sound intrudes the ear canal, vibrates through your temples and shoots down your shoulders until it reaches both knees. By then, your toes are curled, both by the sound and by the anticipation of what sensations lie around the next bend.

Project Nasty whisps onto the 55 Freeway. When the manual transmission dances into third gear, Seely turns with a devilish grin wrapped across his face. "I've gotta give you a little taste," he says. He digs his right foot into the gas pedal. Sparks seem to shoot from Seely's eyes as Project Nasty launches forward and inhales the asphalt ahead. In an instant, the cherry-red Porsche is blasting past Saturday morning traffic as if everyone else is standing still. The speed is overwhelming, but it's nothing compared to the noise. The throaty rattle has transformed, climbing an octave into a divine chorus. It reaches a note that feels as if it could go on forever. Project Nasty sings.

Seely finally shifts up and brings the car to a more serene speed. We had only reached about 80 mph but the sensation caused by its obsessive craftsmanship—its lightness, its brute force, its bare-bones ruthlessness—made it seem like triple digits. And speed is not even Project Nasty's strong suit. There are much faster cars. Hell, there are even faster Porsches that can hit Project Nasty's speeds and deliver better comfort to boot. But few cars deliver the experience this little red cherry bomb has in its back half. Joey Seely created a love ballad to the air-cooled engine. My first thought is that if everyone could experience this, they would never buy new cars.

*

The short jaunt ends as Seely pulls into the modest lot behind a glass, single-story midcentury modern storefront. This is Period Correct, a race-inspired apparel company just down the way in Costa Mesa. Like E-motion Engineering, it calls a nondescript industrial park home. Like Seely, it has an enigmatic leader and legions of followers. Like most Southern California car havens, it is steeped in history.

The building used to be inhabited by Parts Obsolete, a packrat Porsche shop that hoarded components from wheels to motors back when nobody wanted them in the 1970s and '80s. It was run by the Emory family, a lineage of car nuts that ran dealerships, modified customer cars and built brand new ones.

Today, the third-generation Porsche builder Rod Emory is a regular in the SoCal scene for his trademark style: a restored Porsche 356, the automaker's first production vehicle, with its roof chopped and its fenders curved into wild shapes and its tiniest details finished in aluminum or leather or whatever else Emory feels like. His cars are called "Outlaws" because they were once shunned by the Porsche community. Now they're A-list celebrities.

Parts Obsolete left the tiny space in Costa Mesa some years back. The building cycled through a number of tenants before Bryan Calvero came along. Calvero, a 40-year old Filipino-American who grew up in nearby Cerritos, made his name as a fashion designer and distributor alongside his brother, Dennis; the pair built the streetwear brand Crooks & Castles. Its success allowed Calvero to follow other passions—namely cars. Inspired by classic performance and rally racing from the 1980s and '90s, Calvero set about finding the cars that had moved him since childhood. He quickly amassed a collection that includes vintage Porsches, Mercedes and Alfa Romeos. It includes a pristine white BMW E30 M3.

Calvero is also fond of the Renault R5 Turbo and a Lancia Delta Integrale, titans of the European rallying world that were juiced up beyond sanity for the time. The cars are based on the R5 and Delta sedans, objectively boring cars that made surprisingly manic racecars. If the E30 M3 is Exhibit A in the case of Slow Car Fast, the Turbo 2 and Delta Integrale are B1 and B2.

In 2013, Calvero decided to combine his car love with his business acumen and started another clothing brand. He launched Period Correct with an eye toward celebrating vintage motorsport. The name makes reference to a common phrase among car collectors—that is, whether the changes and modifications done to a car are true to its original period, or "period correct." His jackets, sweaters and t-shirts echo the themes and tastes of the 1960s, '70s and '80s motorsport heyday and combine them with modern fits and styles. This is not the palm-tree and woody-station-wagon print on a breezy white polo shirt you'll find in every beach chair at every Americana car show across the country. This is subtle car clothing that is instantly-recognizable to racing fans. The quality is high—sweaters typically run $75 and up while jackets start around $150. And at Southern California car shows, Period Correct is everywhere.

"There was nothing for the true enthusiasts," Calvero says. Period Correct became the first automotive apparel company to wrap decades of history and culture into today's style.

And Calvero has made Period Correct not only reflective of car culture but distinctly part of it, with his Pit Stop car shows. Held in the shop's lot every first Saturday of the month, Pit Stop draws a variety of vintage cars as diverse as the attendees. Many of the cars are classics; others are from more recent eras. But for the most part, the thread that ties them together is that each car at Pit Stop is a reflection of its time. On the day Seely pulls Project Nasty into the lot, there is a grinning black Toyota Supra A80. There are three styles of BMW M3. There is a gaggle of Porsche 911s from all eras, in all conceivable colors.

Even in this group of period correct pieces, Project Nasty stands out. Calvero walks up to the car as it arrives, a big smile on his face as he greets Seely and points him to a reserved spot. Before Seely can step out of the car and slam the feather-light door shut, he is already answering questions from folks beginning to gather. "Nothing on this car is original," Seely says, lovingly, as he guides a group of onlookers around the exterior. After buying the car he immediately replaced the heavy hood and bumper with lightweight composite plastics. He flared the wheel fenders by hand and removed the original roof because he hates sunroofs—they're too heavy.

Seely is on a constant mission to reduce weight. The car is from the 930 era, built between 1974 and 1989, but during that time Porsche used windshields with metal trim. Metal is heavy and, to Seely, heavy is bad. So he installed the windshield from a 964 model instead. He removed the trademark metal badge and had one painted on instead. "I'll always be tweaking it further and further," Seely says. The car is down from its original weight of over 2,600 pounds to less than 2,200 pounds today. When asked how he's been able to produce so much grip from a 35-year old car, Seely takes a second to think. Finally he answers, "Obsession."

Seely is drawn to cars that exude a similar obsession. Of all the cars on display at Period Correct—the canyon carvers and genuine racecars and the rainbow of Porsche 911s—he gravitates toward a tiny white Honda two-door hatchback. At first glance, it is the type of car that would be summarily dismissed by the automotive cognoscenti. The white Honda has a low stance, showy wheels and over-the-top modifications. But Seely keeps finding things to get excited about. He uncharacteristically bounds over to the car, pointing just under its windshield.

"It has a flocked dash!" he shouts, referring to the suede-like texture that covered the dashboard of rally cars to eliminate glare in the driver's view during races. "Who flocks a dash? That's awesome."

Seely has good instincts. The car is more than a white Honda—it is a boxy third-generation Civic from the 1980s stuffed with the giant-killing engine from an Integra Type R[42], a member in good standing of Slow Car Fast. Imagine an old Civic so lovingly prepped and cared for it stands out amid a crowd of Porsches. "It's just clean," Seely says. "I like things that are purpose-built."

The car is the work of Ryan Basseri, the owner of local tuner shop Rywire that has built a reputation for squeezing performance out of cars through their electronics. Basseri greets Seely, the two tuners linked by mutual respect, and begins to show him the finer points of the build. He waxes poetic about the importance of cooling the engine, which is music to Seely's ears.

"Cooling is the biggest thing," he says. "New cars don't last five laps on track before they go into limp mode." The two craftsmen trade war stories, banter about who missed out on the E30 M3 craze more, then say goodbye and part ways.

Seely takes less than five steps before he's greeted by a familiar face. "Bumper's looking good!" booms Jeff Zwart, a renowned automotive photographer and Porsche enthusiast who is also an accomplished racer—he's won the grueling Pike's Peak hill climb eight times, once in a car built by Seely. He's taken notice of the many rock chips, bumps and bruises on Project Nasty and congratulates Seely on driving the car, rather than shelving it. Though they are more than 20 years apart, Zwart and Seely go way back. They've known each other for years and worked closely together on the Luft cars. When Zwart and his wife go out of town, Seely watches their Bernese mountain dog Jezebelle. At the Pit Stop show the pooch runs over to Seely, tongue and tail wagging.

On any given Saturday morning in Southern California there are dozens of car shows like this; free and open to the public, ranging from the pounding American muscle cars and blue-haired Porsche club to the young modded crowd and over-salaried exotic hypercar meet-ups. Consistently though, Pit Stop draws the most interesting group—genuine and curious car-lovers who take their passion seriously yet come to relax and spread love across all automakers. Calvero brings in gourmet coffee and a DJ.

During a Pit Stop meet the previous month I met 19-year old Austin Varco, who drove his BMW M Coupe two hours up from San Diego to enter. As a high schooler, Varco worked extra shifts and saved to afford the car, affectionately known as the Clownshoe. Once the ugly duckling of the car world it soon became a cult classic and is now a bona fide collectible. Varco bought his several weeks before taking his driver's license exam. Since then he's modified it a little and driven it a lot.

"My taste in cars can be categorized by: Analog > Digital," Varco wrote in an email. The M Coupe has a six-speed manual transmission and Varco does most of his own work. The day after we met at Pit Stop he installed a new suspension, and later added a new radiator and bushings. He's raced go-karts since childhood and takes the M Coupe to the track on weekends.

Varco is not the only teenager at Pit Stop. The crowd is almost entirely young and extremely well-versed in the cars on display. They discovered the show, almost universally, through Instagram. They furiously photograph the cars rolling in or hang against the garage doors and share laughs in fitted jogging sweats and expensive sneakers. Inside, the Period Correct collection of hats, t-shirts and jackets is mixed together with vintage automotive magazines, miniature car models and a real-life 1990 Porsche Carrera Cup Car that has raced around the world. Teenagers try not to scratch it as they carry their haul to the register.

"We're a clothing brand first that happens to have a car shop," Calvero says.

*

Zwart and Seely peel off to greet old friends, with Jezebelle trotting closely behind. Back at the Porsche corral are two owners and Seely fans. One, Patrick LaLoggia, watches over his own Porsche 964 911. The car is tagged with E-motion Engineering stickers from nose to tail. He commissioned Seely to tune his 911 for the perfect cruise and routinely visits the shop for check-ups.

"Joey's a suspension genius," LaLoggia says. The 964 has been a labor of love. It is his weekend getaway, his thrills machine and his family hauler. LaLoggia reflects on the value of the time and effort he's put into his project, and nods to the modified BMW M3 beside him. "You don't just go out and buy that—you build it and make it your own. It's more personal."

Seely is across the aisle, chatting with another frequent customer and friend named Lisa Taylor. She is what could be described as a "hoot." Taylor is a ranch owner, horse breeder and, not coincidentally, a Bernese mountain dog breeder. She is not shy. Taylor's car collection includes several Porsches color-matched to her favorite items, be they lipstick, sunglasses or fabrics. Her garage looks like the inside of a Crayola box. Today she has brought to Period Correct a Maritime Blue 997.2 GT3 adorned with her Flying L Racing stickers. In the passenger seat is a matching pair of blue Jimmy Choo stilettos.

"Do I ask too much of you?" she playfully asks Seely, slapping his back and letting out a booming laugh. It soon becomes clear why. She has just taken delivery of the GT3 and wants to take it racing at the local autocross — tomorrow. Which means she wants Seely to set up the suspension today. He chuckles along and insists that Taylor is no bother, but that he isn't sure he wants to spend four hours of his Saturday under her car. He'll think about it, he says, and keeps wandering.

But 20 minutes later, Seely motions that it's time to hop back into Project Nasty.

"Actually I am gonna do that GT3," he says. When one of your biggest customers makes a request there's really only one answer. The car pulls out of Period Correct and Seely waves goodbye to Calvero and the onlookers watching the parade of exiting cars. Seely starts slow, then gives them a burst to post to Instagram. He turns to me and yells over the noise of the engine.

"We need to make a stop!" The car hooks a right, a left and another right before pulling into the empty lot of an office park. In front of us stands a beige building, completely bare. No sign. Nothing in the darkened windows. It looks like the space has been empty for years, but Seely swears this is the place. He stands next to the car for several minutes, scrolling his phone and waiting.

Suddenly the front door pops open. Handshakes and hugs are exchanged. We are ushered inside one of the largest and best-known aftermarket performance companies. They keep the outside of the building intentionally boring and I'm asked to keep the brand name to myself. The strategy continues even inside. For a brand synonymous with acceleration, excitement and power, the empty cubicles and unadorned walls seem more appropriate for a regional data-entry branch. Even that might have a motivational poster or two.

Seely picks up the equipment he needs and heads back to the car. It's going to be a longer Saturday than he expected. On the entry to the freeway he digs into the throttle of Project Nasty. The car sucks to the ground as it screams across the on ramp. Even from the passenger seat, the connection between the steering wheel and the tires is profound, almost telepathic. Modern supercars achieve this feeling through computers and microprocessors. Seely creates it by hand and tests it through the vibration sent to his butt.

When Seely arrives back at E-motion, the Porsche is already waiting for him. He plays Tetris with the other cars in the garage, moving them outside into the parking lot to create a path for the GT3 to drive it onto the lift. After a morning of brutal runs in the intentionally-unaccommodating Project Nasty, a short ride in the GT3—currently one of the most extreme sports cars on the planet—feels like the back of a Lincoln Towncar.

Seely hoists the GT3 into the air and arranges his tools. All over his shop are testaments to what he's accomplished in the past. There is a plaque atop one filing cabinet commemorating his trips to the 24 Hours of Le Mans. The team, a partnership between Petersen Motorsports and White Lightning Racing, won the GT2 class in 2004 and finished second in 2005. Seely served as chief mechanic. Inside the plaque are his boarding pass, his Eurail ticket, his access pass—still in its lanyard—and bracelet. A portrait of the team's three drivers, who each autographed it, is at the top. Jörg Bergmeister, who would go on to win the ALMS Driver's Championship five times; Timo Bernhard, who would win ALMS three times and take two overall victories at Le Mans; and Patrick Long—a murderer's row of racing pedigree putting their faith in Seely.

When asked to name the most talented driver he's ever worked with, Seely pauses for a beat. "Pat," he says. "Legend."

When the Porsche is finally in the air, Seely sets himself beside it and turns Pandora to the Radiohead station on his Bluetooth speaker. The electric strums of "Optimistic" begin to waft through the garage. He leans against a red Craftsman cabinet and gingerly holds his third Americano of the day. Seely takes a sip, his eyes fixated on something straight ahead. I follow the gaze to see where his attention is focused, but there's nothing. He's not looking at the car, he's looking through it. Maybe toward the plaques and trophies on the wall. Maybe toward the stand-up paddleboards hanging on hooks that have long since dried. Maybe toward a future project he has in mind, or the successor to Project Nasty that remains to be sketched. Maybe toward the work laid out before him or the ultimate Porsche he'll build one day. He releases a deep sigh. "Alright," he says. He gets to work.

Chapter VI: The New Car Stars

Matt Farah's phone is dying. It's just past 9:00 a.m. on a bright Sunday morning in April and the 35-year-old writer and automotive personality keeps pulling out his iPhone 6 with its cracked screen to check the battery. "Fifteen percent," he says. "Not good."

Farah will need the phone. He's standing in the middle of the most highly-anticipated annual shows in the Southern California car scene, Luftgekühlt, surrounded by 10,000 people in a confined space—many of whom will recognize him on-sight from his many television appearances, YouTube videos and podcast episodes. His media company, The Smoking Tire, has amassed millions of followers across multiple platforms. And at 6-foot-2, 260 pounds[43] and a cue-ball shaved head, Farah is easy to find. Over the next two hours he will be asked to shake hands, take selfies, write down numbers, schedule appointments and pull up pictures at a moment's notice. Farah also needs the phone to get home. His car is parked at a friend's place about an hour away.

For now, though, Farah is in a good mood. He stands with a collection of friends that includes Spike Ferensten, the comedian and podcast host who made his name writing the "Soup Nazi" episode of *Seinfeld* among others, and Nic Cuarta, founder of the automotive-themed roasters Beeline Coffee. This year's rendition of Luftgekühlt places roughly 500 Porsches in a lumber yard in Torrance. Farah and his friends are standing inside an open-air warehouse, next to a block of raw lumber about 15 feet high, staring at a priceless lineup.

To the left is a white-and-yellow 908K Works Short Tail raced at Spa in 1968 by the Porsche factory team[44]. To the right is a stunning silver 804 open-wheel racer, the only Porsche to ever win a Formula One race back in 1962[45]. There are multiple 934/5 racecars with glorious winged sideskirts sprung as wide as the rules would allow.[46] There are championship winners from Can-

Am and Le Mans and the International Motor Sports Association. There is a life-sized model of a 911 made of wooden slats, an ornate steampunk-inspired 911 with copper accents and red quilted leather and Jerry Seinfeld's personal 356 Gmünd—so named because the earliest Porsches were built at the company's facility in Gmünd, Germany before relocating to Zuffenhausen in 1949[47].

In German, the word *Luftgekühlt* means "air-cooled." It's a reference to the engines Porsche made that used giant aluminum fans to reduce heat by sending air over the cylinder heads. The company built nearly all of its engines with this technique for more than 50 years, until the introduction of the new "water-cooled" 911, widely known as the 996, in 1998[48]. Since all Porsches are now water-cooled, the old air-cooled ones are hot commodities. There are many reasons for the explosion in interest for air-cooled Porsches—they're lighter, easier to work on and better sounding than modern ones. They also harken back to a purer era, when sports cars didn't make much in the way of power but delivered a mechanical connection to the driver that has since been engineered out of modern cars. Air-cooled is a religion to many enthusiasts. Luftgekühlt is Mecca.

The group ventures out of the shaded area and into a barrage of sunlight. Here there are even more standout vehicles, arranged in a throughline to follow the progress of Porsche history, hopped up on wooden platforms to signify their elevated status. Ferensten peels off to inspect a crystal blue 356 Speedster and is quickly lost. Farah gravitates toward a 1973 Carrera RS, one of the most hallowed road cars in Porsche history, draped in iconic Dalmatian Blue paint. "This thing is"—here, Farah's voice changes to a higher pitch than you would think he is capable—"*extremely* sick!"

Farah doesn't linger too long in any one spot. In jeans and blue suede Pumas, he constantly paces and sways, his eyes darting to catch an old friend or a treasured car lurking in a corner. Even in conversation he gradually moves away from the person he's talking to, seemingly without noticing it, which creates a sort of gravitational pull on the person to keep moving toward him. Every few minutes he sneaks a pull from the wood-grained marijuana pen in his hand and half-discreetly sends the smoke into the sky.

The crowd of attendees, like the cars on display, is vast and diverse. The beauty of Luft is that is combines high-class Porsches with once-sacrilegious custom Porsches and presents them in the same light. Zero-mile garage queens in a lumber yard. Priceless Le Mans winners alongside modified rebels from RWB and Rod Emory Outlaws. Meticulously pedicured Singers downwind of sun-bleached 914s with mismatched wheels. The only thing tying them all together being air-cooled engines and the coat of arms on the hood. Similarly, the people are from all different backgrounds and age ranges. Many are young and dressed in L.A. clean casual fashion, like they've stepped out of a Zara ad. Not your typical Porsche owner. But they're drawn to the air-cooled trend, and because he's like them, they're drawn to Farah.

Farah shoots glances over the heads of people around him. There are waves and waves of cars to see. Besides, he's starting to get noticed. Soon it's difficult for the group to take five consecutive steps without stopping to wait for him to finish a new conversation. One fan simply offers a handshake. Another says he wishes Farah would continue his trademark "One Take" videos on YouTube, where he drives enthusiasts' personal cars, often heavily modified, and offers on-the-spot critiques from behind the wheel along a twisty road. Farah was already a fast-rising celebrity in automotive circles, but One Takes made him a star. He offered fair, leveled critiques of Mitsubishi Starions in the same manner he would review a factory-fresh McLaren, a rarity among automotive critics. The idea that anyone with a homebuilt creation could find professional feedback from a serious, respected journalist and have the experience documented to show off was a novel one. If young enthusiasts are truly brand agnostic and value diversity in their cars, the One Take series is a treasure trove. Farah gave equal importance to a 2002 Saab as a 1972 Mercedes sedan and a beat-to-hell 1996 Mustang GT.

The best episodes are when Farah is stuck in truly bad cars. "It looks horrible, but kind of funny horrible, and it drives really horrible, but like a good kind of horrible," he said in a 2014 video[49] behind the wheel of a diesel-powered Volkswagen Jetta converted to a pickup truck with razor-thin rear tires. The entirety of the episode Farah vacillates between uncontrollable laughter and genuine terror.

"It's just, it's not good… but I'm having a really good time."

After making more than 600 of the videos and tens of millions of views in just three years, Farah announced in 2018 he would retire the series. An outpouring from fans convinced him to continue, but with writer Zack Klapman taking over as host.

"Zack is going to keep it going," he tells the pleading fan. Farah just couldn't do it anymore. The videos required minimal investment and editing, but took weeks to arrange and required a lot of moving parts. Farah often scheduled three cars per morning shoot—once as many as seven. Guests were sometimes flakey, or exaggerated what they had. Frankly, it was a little dangerous. "You only have control of the first 18 inches of this car," Farah said in the 2014 video about the frightening Volkswagen. "Everything else happens without your knowledge or consent."

More than anything, though, Farah found One Take repetitive. "I got tired of doing the same thing over and over and over and over and over," he says while browsing at Luft.

It speaks to the problem many personalities are finding on YouTube. As the platform enters its second decade, there is already an infinite amount of content with more uploaded to the site every day. A recent study found that five hours of new video posts on YouTube every second[50]. Collectively, viewers watch more than one billion hours of content every day[51]. And to keep up with that demand, the site's algorithm pushes accounts that upload most frequently to the top. Quality is rewarded by loyal viewers, but quantity is rewarded with placement on the front page. You can't grow to reach the former without committing to the latter.

The One Take videos were a quick way to produce consistent output without a tremendous amount of time and money. They also performed well, usually generating between 100,000 and 300,000 views per video from The Smoking Tire's 825,000 subscribers. The occasional One Take surpasses half a million views. Interest isn't the problem.

The problem is it gets exhausting. The YouTube machine demands content and pays a relative pittance in return. It's an imperfect science, but Google's Adsense system doles out a couple hundred dollars per each 100,000 views[52]. That comes to a few thousand dollars per million views, which isn't a lot of money for creators with a huge audience. If output slows down, YouTube demotes the account and views drop sharply.

"It became about volume," Farah says. "I was about to have an aneurysm."

I heard similar refrains from others who are active in the world of automotive social media, with YouTube in particular pressing them to always produce more and more. The vlogger Emelia Hartford told me she got her start by making videos about the car work she was already doing anyway. But when she quickly grew an audience, the pressure to produce increased. "I had to keep the content interesting," Hartford said.

"It's constantly trying to find the next thing. What do people want to see? I was trying to maintain and continue to do my best."

One of her strategies for coming up with new content was a series where she drove other people's cars in search of her next build project. That way she could test the water and gauge viewer response before committing long-term. Hartford kept up a breakneck pace of about three videos per week for the next year. But in spring 2019 she took a short sabbatical from YouTube and returned stressing the importance of focusing on her mental and physical health. By the middle of the summer Hartford ramped up her output again.

Farah's solution was to find ways outside of YouTube to keep his brand growing. Since stepping away from One Take, he's spending more time contributing to *Road & Track* and posting regularly to Instagram, where he has more than 200,000 followers and a huge engagement rate without the hassle of YouTube.

Farah first burst onto the scene in the mid-2000s as the business development director for the New York Motor Club[53], a group of east coast enthusiasts who made their exotic vehicles available for other members to drive on long distance rallies. Farah filmed the club's exploits—a Skittles-colored stream of various supercars screaming through upstate New York at triple-digit speeds, its drivers laughing at one another for getting pulled over—and posted them on YouTube as the burgeoning site began attracting swarms of young viewers.

Recognizing the audience for automotive content, Farah started his first YouTube channel Garage419 in 2007, where he developed a reputation for enthusiastic first-hand reports from corners of the automotive world that were normally left in the dark. Autocrossing, street drifting and desert racing all found a home alongside industry news and motorsports coverage.

In 2009, Farah left New York for Los Angeles and shed the Garage419 moniker. He started a new venture as a YouTube page called The Smoking Tire. In the past decade the account has posted more than 900 videos with over 270 million views. Farah and his team filmed two documentary films, *All Cars Go To Heaven* and *All Cars Go To Heaven II*, about driving used cars through the wilderness—sometimes equipped for the journey, sometimes not. He's also willing to push the boundaries for kicks. Farah has boasted about the number of speeding tickets he racked up and once posted audio of talking his way out of one. He listed his DeLorean on the auction site Bring a Trailer and announced the results live on his podcast, audibly fretting about low bidding. It eventually sold for a strong $52,000[54].

These are not gimmicks so much as a personality switch that Farah can't flip off. Driving cars is simply who Matt Farah is. He has the word "Clutch" tattooed on his left calf and "Gas" tattooed on his right. Few can claim to match the cavernous automotive knowledge that Farah has. While not an engineer, Farah has an encyclopedic memory of his experiences. Considering the number of fan vehicles he has driven, plus a consistent stream of press vehicles from manufacturers and his own rotating stable, it's difficult to imagine a person on Earth who has driven more cars than Matt Farah.

Farah wasn't the first person to post car videos online, but he was the first to launch an automotive lifestyle brand of his own using YouTube as the centerpiece. He's also the savviest at linking his followers across platforms. There are myriad ways to interact with Farah. He has loyal followings on YouTube, Facebook, Twitter and Instagram, and will answer questions sent via those platforms on his podcast. He built two podcast studios out of his Culver City office, one for small groups and one for larger ones, and leveraged his YouTube following by broadcasting the podcasts live on video. He was an early adopter of YouTube's Super Chat feature, which allows viewers to shoot their comments and questions to the top of the feed if they pay an amount of their choosing. So far the feature brings in about $50 per episode, but Farah says if that figure surpasses what he makes on ads for each podcast he'll eliminate ads from his podcasts entirely.

Podcasting may be the thing Farah is most skilled at. He's a natural on radio, with insightful questions of his guests and the ability to carry a conversation with natural rhythm for several minutes at a time. At least in part, this can be attributed to his influences outside of the car world. Farah has cited Howard Stern, the comedian Bill Burr and especially *The Opie & Anthony Show* that ran for more than 19 years on AM radio and then SiriusXM satellite. Farah briefly tried stand-up comedy early in his career, but in podcasting he's found an outlet for his love of talking cars, his sometimes bombastic and off-color jokes and his natural charisma that makes guests and listeners alike feel welcome.

It is no coincidence that as Farah wound down his grueling YouTube schedule in early 2018, he doubled The Smoking Tire podcast output to two per week. Each episode brought in about 140,000 to 150,000 listeners on the old schedule. Since doubling output Farah sees about 165,000 total listens per week.

All of this media makes Farah one of the most influential figures in car culture today. There are other automotive presenters on YouTube with massive followings—the drifter Hartford has quickly amassed more than 300,000 subscribers; vlogger and exotic stable-owner Alejandro Salomondrin surpassed 1.6 million; and car-quirk aficionado Doug Demuro will soon pass 3 million—but in an era where more young people are turning to YouTube to learn about the world, Farah's face is one that budding enthusiasts simply can't avoid.

"If you have ever watched a car review on the internet, there's a good chance it was starring Matt Farah," writes the YouTube channel Gears and Gasoline[55].

Farah has written regular featured columns for several popular sites, including *The Drive* and *Road & Track*, but since he isn't exclusive to any one publication, he has the leeway to express opinions that would never make their way onto the pages of legacy magazines.

Two of his views in particular have been frequent topics on the podcast: factory cars are too fast; and there are too many rich people[56]. Even if you don't agree, Farah's willingness to put unpopular opinions on the table makes The Smoking Tire podcast a breath of fresh air in automotive media.

Farah is also hard at work on his first foray into the car-collecting business: building a state-of-the-art storage facility that will stow valuable cars for a monthly fee. It will have easy access for customers, round the clock security, climate control and the best sprinkler system money can buy. Ground had just broken on the site as Farah perused the grounds at Luftgekühlt.

"All is right in the world," Farah answers every time someone asks how he's doing. "Just got my building permits." You get the sense that the garage represents a next step for Farah. After more than a decade of shooting, hosting and editing videos for the Internet, a reprieve seems around the corner—if he could just get the damn thing built. The facility, Westside Collector Car Storage, is scheduled to open in fall 2019. He's also recently engaged, to his fiancée Hannah, and is looking forward to married life. Farah is too obsessed with car culture to step away—the Instagram, podcasts and writing jobs could continue in perpetuity without much trouble—but it's possible car enthusiasts may soon be seeing less of his face and reading more of his words.

Back at Luft, the group continues on, adding new members as Farah runs into people he knows from various branches of the car world: Matthew Ivanhoe, a private sales broker who is displaying a zero-mile Schuppan 962 that looks as if someone built a racecar sponsored by the Death Star; Sam Fankuchen, a vintage 4x4 collector and startup investor who is also Farah's neighbor; the creative directors of the competing wheel companies HRE and Fifteen52. If he's not being stopped by a friend, he's being stopped by a complete stranger.

"Dude, if you think this is bad," Farah says, "SEMA is a nightmare."

After a rare 12 consecutive steps in which he's not approached, Farah runs into a friend who has switched jobs and now works at a highly-esteemed brand in the automotive world. "Can you get me into a car?" he asks. "Your PR rep is a great person but won't let me drive one for some goddamn reason."

Of course, comes the reply.

"See? If the PR person says no, just wait," Farah says. "A friend will work there eventually!" He lets out a signature boom that can best be described as a gut-cackle. Farah's network has grown to the point that its tentacles reach into whatever connection he needs next. "Just wait!"

The group moves on. Farah reunites with Ferensten, who has brought along his podcast co-host, an area attorney named Paul Zuckerman who once litigated against Toyota over the automaker's unintended acceleration scandal and resulting class-action lawsuit. Farah started his day by parking in Zuckerman's hangar at the Santa Monica Airport. Then, realizing that Zuckerman's vintage Alfa Romeo Giulia was the only available car with more than two seats, the three of them stuffed inside and headed down the 405 Freeway for Luft. They were halfway to Torrance when Ferensten realized he left the tickets at home. The trio only got through the gates when Farah called Long and asked him to chat with gate security.

Anticipating that they'll soon get separated again, and that Farah's phone is about to die, and that Farah will eventually need his car back, Zuckerman suggests Farah write down the key code to his hangar. A pen is produced. Farah starts to write on the palm of his hand, then changes his mind and pulls out a dollar bill. He writes the code above George Washington's head, stuffs the bill back into his pocket and sets off.

The rest of the event is more gawking, more handshakes, more friends. When the group wanders to the far reaches of the lumber yard with no shade in sight, Farah says he could use some water. An Arrowhead bottle magically appears from the arm of a passerby. Laughing, Farah courteously dumps it into his mouth in a waterfall motion and continues on.

*

In 2017, Farah bought a 1987 Porsche 911 SC, painted purple with a giant whale tail spoiler, that he is having converted in a "Safari" build. There are few things hotter in the automotive world than a Safari Porsche. It's a term used to describe a Porsche 911, usually of the air-cooled variety, converted for off-road use. Safari Porsches are all made in the vein of the 953—a heavily modified 911 built to compete in the 1984 Paris-Dakar Rally[57]. Porsche made three cars in the same white and blue two-tone paint with red and yellow striping. One of them won the race outright. The cars boasted advanced four-wheel drive technology that helped the automaker develop its world-beating 959 the following year—some of which would also go on to compete in Dakar. Safari builds follow this basic format. Sports car, lifted suspension, off-road tires and rally lights. Engine upgrades are frequent but not mandatory.

In the first few months of 2018, a 1991 Porsche 911 Safari sold for $200,964 on Bring A Trailer, followed by an '83 911SC Safari that garnered $142,000[58]. Whether those are well-sorted cars or flash-in-the-pan sales that will cause the trend to flame out is difficult to tell. For his part, Farah is calling in the big guns. Engine upgrades will be performed by BBi Autosport, Joey Seely's former shop. The Safari modifications are assigned to Leh Keen, a professional racecar driver who builds rally-ready Porsches out of his garage in Georgia.

Farah has been desperate to have a Keen Safari car ever since he reviewed one in 2016. At Luft, Farah runs into Keen, who flew out to L.A. to attend and wears a white t-shirt screen printed with an image of a black Porsche 911 speeding away from an explosion that fills the frame. Farah correctly identifies the shot from the 1995 film *Bad Boys* starring Will Smith and Martin Lawrence. Keen made it himself. But more and more these days he's making Porsches.

Keen, 35, built a career racing Porsches across the world, but especially in American sports car series. He made 144 starts over 11 seasons, notching 14 wins at famed placed such as Sebring, Watkins Glen and Laguna Seca. Keen also raced at the 24 Hours of Le Mans three times, taking second in class with a Ferrari F430 GTC in 2010[59].

In 2013, he started the Keen Project, producing rally-inspired Porsches. Keen is looking to capture the magic of the 953 with his creations. The first was his personal car, a tangerine 1981 911 SC[60] with protective skid plates and a ducktail spoiler that can be seen mobbing through the woods at a sideways pitch all over the Internet. The car makes only 200 horsepower—less than a pittance in 2018 parlance. But the balance, feedback and response engineered into the car by Keen, even with off-road modifications that add weight and increase drag, have turned anyone who drives it into a believer.

Farah can hardly contain his excitement when talking about his future car. "Mine will probably be here next year," he glows. An important aspect of the 911 Safari is nostalgia, a celebration of the time-specific period from which these cars first debuted. Keen's personal car features a red, black and white-striped cloth interior that is stunningly '80s. Farah already picked his own interior print and he races to pull out his phone—now nearing 5 percent battery life—to show me the fabric. It's a flat gray base color with laser-thin diagonal dashes of neon blue, green and orange. Farah calls it "L.A. city bus seats." It looks like the carpet of an airport.

That's all part of the charm for Farah. Once the car is complete he plans to take it off-road frequently, to the many trails, deserts and dry lake beds within a morning's drive of Los Angeles. It's one of the few driving experiences he hasn't spent much time with and he's already envisioning media he can share with his fans. 911 Safaris are among the hottest automotive trends in the country—both Dropped Alfa and Rallyata were heavily influenced by the idea—but when Matt Farah begins to post regularly, shooting rooster tails of dirt 20 feet into the air over 100 mph in the lawless Mojave Desert, it's difficult to see the Safari theme not launching to new levels.

*

After a reprieve from the beating sun in the Luftgekühlt beer garden, a few more selfies and a new group of friends, Farah is ready to leave. It's been a whirlwind. He found a ride back to his car and with 3 percent battery life remaining heads out to meet the driver over text. Farah managed to see a slight majority of the cars on display in his two hours at the show.

But afterward, the part that sticks with me most is watching him engage with his fans. It may be cumbersome being Matt Farah at a car show, but like on his podcast, or in the One Takes, he makes people feel comfortable talking to him. At one point a young couple approached him, the man shaking his hand and the woman offering gratitude. "You're teaching me to drive stick," she says. They told Farah that they dug up one of his old instructional videos to watch his technique. "It's fun, it's going really well."

Farah's eyes light up. Here is a person discovering a new automotive experience through media he created. He stops and spends several minutes asking questions about the test car, inquiring about the process and offering advice. "You should learn to drive stick on a shitty car, like a rented Ford Focus," he says. "That way you don't worry about messing up."

The rest of his group begins to drift off. Farah stays with the couple until it's finally time to move on. The sun is beating on his bare head. He apologizes for running, shakes hands again and hurries to catch up. After jogging a few steps he turns in the direction of the couple.

"Good luck driving stick!" he bellows over the crowd, thrusting a thumbs-up high into the air. "You can do it!"

Chapter VII: Acquired Taste

There is one word that will instantly put a gleaming smile on the face of almost any young automotive enthusiast. It's a word that represents an era and aesthetic gone by. It's a word that at first impression sounds like a mockery dripping in Millennial post-ironic smarm, but on second glance it holds a genuine appreciation and passion. In the car world, it's less of an event and more of a movement—and it's growing all the time.

Radwood.

"Honestly that was the most fun car show I've been to in… I don't even know how long," said Kim, the industry analyst, of the traveling '80s and '90s inspired car show. "There was such positive energy there, so many people having a good time. This was a celebration, not a competition. Did you see the BMX demo?"

There are those who see declining interest in muscle cars and classic American iron, who see falling attendance at traditional car shows, and take it all to mean that car culture is dying. But they just don't know where to look. Radwood is the answer. And it's the future of car culture.

Radwood is a roving celebration of cars that are traditionally unloved. It includes vehicles from the model years 1980 to 1999, an era of auto history typified to many by underpowered plastic cost-cutters struggling to shake off the chains of malaise. But the real Radwood definition is less rigid than that. Radwood is built around an aesthetic and attitude not restricted to cars, but encompassing the roots of geeky computer nerd-dom and skateboarding counter-culture. People wear denim and neon and pastel and carry boom boxes. The Radwood website describes the inspiration as a "bodacious era." It isn't for everybody, but it is for a lot of people.

"It's one of those things that makes sense after the fact," says Bryan McQueen, a co-host of the popular automotive podcast *Driving While Awesome*, one of several factions that organizes Radwood events. The name is a play on the Goodwood Festival of Speed, an annual display of motorsport history and heritage held on the 12,000-acre Goodwood House estate in West Sussex, England. Goodwood is sponsored by Mastercard. Tickets run $350 a pop. By comparison, Radwood is like a backyard house party. Tickets are $10 for admission and $25 to show a car. Mullets and Spandex are encouraged. But there is no less passion for cars.

There have been about a dozen Radwoods since the first one in 2017. Shows have been help up and down California and stretching east to Atlanta and Philadelphia, with a dozen others planned through 2019. There's even a Radwood planned to be held at Goodwood. Each one celebrates not only the cars of the '80s and '90s, but also the culture. Attendees dress up and carry aluminum briefcases and enormous cell phones and make jokes about cocaine. Punk and ska music pump from the main speakers. The trophies are Nintendo cartridges mounted on plaques. There are skateboard half-pipes and preppy sweaters and cassette tapes—lots of cassette tapes. Each show draws thousands of attendees. Tickets to the Los Angeles show in late 2017 sold out weeks in advance. The UK show sold out even faster.

"It's not surprising at all that people would be amped on this timeframe," McQueen told me. "The whole aspect of people dressing up is super fun and now people are buying cars just to come to the event. It's an approachable theme. You have a place to respect these models that would otherwise sit on the side."

There are several keys to the success of Radwood. First, it traffics in nostalgia for the exact era that Millennials grew up in. It attracts the kinds of cars that they loved and their parents hated or didn't understand. And as Millennials are coming of age and starting to earn disposable income, it's cars from this era that they remember most and are affordable to buy. Some of the fastest growing classic cars in value are Japanese imports like the Mazda RX-7 and Toyota Supra[61], as well as pony cars like the Fox-body Mustang and fourth-generation Camaro, or Group B-inspired Euros like the Audi Quattro and

Renault Turbo 2[62]. Even in their time, these were not generally regarded as particularly fast cars, but they fit the "slow car fast" philosophy like hot pink leggings.

Second, celebrating a specific time period through the lens of cars opens the show to people who don't necessarily consider themselves automotive enthusiasts. I attended Radwood L.A. with two friends who are decidedly not car people. But the atmosphere of era-specific pop culture and design creates a background with which to appreciate the cars on display. It's an experience. Even if you don't like cars, there's something irresistible about a *Back to the Future* Delorean, the menace of a Buick Grand National or the charisma of a rigged-out Mistubishi Delica camper van.

Radwood is also more of a small-scale festival than a traditional car show. There is a lot to do and a lot to see, but also places to escape, take a break, grab a bite or a beer. There's a dance floor. The show takes the user experience into account.

"Radwood was definitely a celebration of lifestyle and nostalgia over speed," Kim said. The traditional refrain is that car shows aren't about cars; they're about people. But until now that hasn't really been true. Whether it's the hoity-toity excess of a concours (a fancy word for "car show with overpriced admission") or the exotic buffet of a typical Cars and Coffee, at most car shows there is not much to do or see besides the cars. Compared to them, Radwood is Car Coachella.

"We get to play a role of participating in the new generation of enthusiasts," McQueen told me. "There's the establishment of all the classic car guys and pre-existing ideas of what a car show is and what types of cars are allowed in it. Part of what we're able to do is shift that forward a bit. I'm super humble about our place in it because we're just a product of it, but we're able to bring a voice to a car show that may not just be standing around and polishing your muscle car. Let's rethink it and do what matters to us."

*

Radwood is one of a kind, but it's part of a growing number of car shows that are trending away from static viewing and toward interactive celebration of an associated lifestyle and culture. Whether it's the celebration of shitty cars at Concours d'LeMons, the track-focused music festival at Gridlife, or to a lesser extent the hyper-specific theme and style of Luftgekühlt, car shows and events are not existing despite a growing disinterest from Millennials. Rather, they're bending toward the changing, morphing, evolving preferences of younger enthusiasts. And the events are successful because of it.

"I think it's allowing avenues of discovery and inviting people into our world as enthusiasts and hobbyists and fans," said Patrick Long, the racecar driver and Luftgekühlt founder. We spoke over the phone just days after Luft at the lumber yard.

"You have something so aspirational and a product that reflects success or luxury," Long said. "When you distill that and peel it back and make it accessible and welcome new people in, they're allowed to learn at their pace and discover what actually brought us all to be fans."

Long breaks it down in a way that clearly delineates the current wave of car events from the old guard. Of course, all car shows are about gawking at cars. That won't change. But what Luft, Radwood and other events add is a level of warmth and accessibility that appeals to both hardcore fans and non-car people alike. By taking cars out of their normal element, or adding new elements like wider cultural appreciation, the show embraces people who don't share an enthusiast's affinity for the cars themselves.

The resulting effect is a breakdown of traditional car show barriers and hierarchies. Luft and Radwood are exceptional because they focus on cars that have traditionally not been celebrated widely. In the past, car shows have worked hard to exclude others that weren't deemed worthy—whether they were cars from what was considered a lesser brand; or attendees who weren't considered as passionate, dedicated or hardcore as everyone else. Opening the doors to all marks a landmark shift in U.S. automotive culture.

"There's a lot of awesome stuff out there from trucks to cars to dune buggies. We just like it all," McQueen said. "At a Ferrari show, Best in Show is the most expensive, most rare, in best condition. And that keeping up with the Joneses culture feels very competitive. So if you have an Alfa Romeo instead, there's a hierarchy and class system. For us and the events we do, it feels like there's more respect for everything."

Part of what has given rise to this broadened appeal is social media, specifically Instagram. The power and influence "The Gram" now wields in shaping car culture is difficult to overstate. The app is flooded with pictures and videos of cars. There are thriving cultures and sub-cultures and micro-cultures that now flourish and grow at breakneck speed. The sheer amount of content, combined with the instantaneous nature of posting, commenting and connecting with other interested people through hashtags and the Stories feature, allows users to dive as deep as they want into any automotive community as hard and as quickly as they want. This opens up a world of cars to people who otherwise may not have been bothered to pick up a car magazine, or even visit a website. But they can easily tap and scroll through Instagram.

It also doesn't hurt that the events themselves are visually stunning Instagram bait. The outfits, the concerts, the lumber yard—all of it creates an idyllic backdrop for photos that rake in the likes. At the time of this writing, the #Luft5 hashtag included 8,600 photos from a single event. Combined, #Luftgekühlt and #Luftgekuhlt have more than 250,000 images attached to it. The #Radwood tag has more than 25,000 with smaller factions broken up across its many events, and #Gridlife has more than 125,000 posts. Spend any time on a visual medium like Instagram and it won't take long to figure out how these events have gained so much prominence in such a short timeframe.

Two nights before Luft 5, the 2018 event, organizers held an invitation-only pre-party at the Petersen Automotive Museum in the trendy Mid-Wilshire neighborhood of Los Angeles. The event was to kick off "Luft weekend" and honor legends from Porsche past. The Petersen traditionally goes to great lengths to recognize L.A. car sub-cultures and reflect them alongside the more highly esteemed factions of automotive culture. Notably, it has exhibited lowriders alongside priceless pre-war classics and Hollywood film cars. So the museum's recognition and celebration of Luft, a decidedly Los Angeles event, not only speaks to its growth and success, but also represents an official acceptance into higher automotive circles by the concours cognoscenti. Tickets to the kickoff were $120 each[63]—more than four times the price of Luft tickets themselves.

Joey Seely and Jeff Zwart were there. The event also welcomed Porsche icons like Le Mans winner Hurley Haywood and designer Howie Idelson to be interviewed onstage by Long, who headed straight from the party to the Luft site to begin prepping for the show in the morning.

After the talk I caught up with Zwart. He's been involved with the planning and managing of Luft since the inaugural event in 2014, with two dozen cars in the parking lot of a motorcycle apparel shop. "The vibe that Howie and Patrick created has become such a unique story in the car world," Zwart told me. "We're not just parking cars, we're telling stories."

He acknowledged that the contrasting mixture of Porsches both high-brow and low-brow had contributed to the growth of Luft.

"It's been nice because it seemed like the enthusiasm for Porsche was falling off with the new cars and it had been forgotten for awhile," Zwart said. "This type of event really bridges the past with the present in a way that for some reason is cool.

"I think when you look at the crowd it's not the typical Porsche crowd. It's a very cosmopolitan, very hipster, very blended viewpoint that people are bringing to it. The way it comes across and the presentation is what makes it feel different."

He's right. At Luft, as I was getting ready to leave, I filed into line at a booth to receive a free event poster. Huddled against a mass of people longing for shade, I noticed a man standing next to me holding a fresh copy of the official hardcover book documenting the history of Luftgekühlt. How much did it cost, I asked. "Oh," he said. "A hundred-twenty[64]." I must have made a face. "I know, it's a lot, but I have the other three," he said.

The pre-party at the Petersen had elements of culture clash as well. There was a drive-in car show with air-cooled Porsche models of all shapes and eras, from factory-clean 911s to track-tuned monsters from mad-scientist companies Ruf and Gemballa. Video projectors plastered vintage racing onto the wall of the museum and a row of racing simulators gave people the chance to beat each other's virtual lap times in the new Porsche GT2RS. Music pumped from behind the open bars.

Of course the museum opened its doors as well. The top level featured cars you were scared to breathe on, like a pristine Ferrari 125S and a dramatic 857 Sport—both from 1955. Below that the ground level was occupied by The Porsche Effect, a holy celebration of Porsche history that traced the brand's history from concepts and drawings to fully realized racecars. There was an ultra-rare 911 GT1 and a race-winning RS Spyder. The hallowed 953 rally car, the holy grail for Safari lovers, still wore dirt from its victory in the 1985 Paris-Dakar off-road race. There's an element to the Petersen that merges with the theme of Luft: combining high and low, priceless and worthless, clean and dirty. Celebrating it all. But an esteemed museum like the Petersen can't go all the way. There are other events for that.

*

Gridlife is one of the car events that truly marks a new guard. Each year there are five Gridlife events and two festivals. The festivals take place over a three-day weekend at Road Atlanta in Georgia and Gingerman Raceway in Michigan. There are musical performances, camping and partying. There are car shows, driving lessons on the track, time attack competitions and drifting demos from pro racers. You can come and go, drive or party. Basically, you can get as involved as you want. Tickets start at $55 for the entire weekend.

In 2018, Gridlife teamed up with Radwood for the first time. Entrance to Gridlife South at Road Atlanta bought you a ticket to an adjoining Radwood show, which drew an eclectic group of '80s and '90s cars from the surrounding Georgia area, plus other Gulf states and up the Eastern seaboard. Gridlife and Radwood might celebrate different eras and driving styles, but just as Radwood spotlights an era that has typically been unloved and dismissed, Gridlife celebrates cars that make next-door neighbors grimace and monocle-wearing judges squirm. They're Mustangs with too much power, BMWs with too many mods and Hondas with too many wings, fins and stickers. They're homemade, they're garish and they're fast as fuck.

At the 2018 festival, William Au-Yeung, the owner of a Civic Si with fantastical downforce add-ons, shattered Gingerman's record for production vehicles with a 1:23.775 lap[65]. More than 500 drivers raced or took lessons on the track over the weekend. There are a number of ways to compete, from single lap times to a tournament bracket knockout that combines time attack with wheel-to-wheel racing. There are a ton of classes and a huge variety of cars.

Thousands of people go to each Gridlife event—often the number exceeds 10,000[66], and a huge percentage is made of Millennials or younger. There are hardcore racers, builders and enthusiasts. To others, it's their first car show. This is the new car culture, and Gridlife feels like where shows are headed. On the track there's a cacophony of focused machines ripping through apexes and shattering course records. Off the track there's a throbbing crowd while Ludacris or Killer Mike or The Cool Kids boom through speakers as the sun goes down. It's not a move away from cars. It's car culture with an emphasis on culture. For the first time, car culture is actually about the people.

"Interests are diversifying and people don't want to spend all their time doing one thing," said Heyward Wagner, an organizer with the Sports Car Club of America, the most esteemed amateur motorsports organization in the U.S. The SCCA will turn 75 years old in 2019. Since its inception it's introduced countless young people to the sport, launching the careers of many pro drivers. Others stay amateur and race for decades.

Now the SCCA is adapting. Wagner is trying to lead a renaissance of sorts, away from the strict, timed structure of its traditional events and toward a more welcoming and inclusive style. In 2014 the SCCA created a new department of experiential programs and named Wagner director[67]. He's a frequent Gridlife attendee and sees it as a harbinger of the future. "Less and less Americans are interested in having 'a' thing," he told me. "It's about being able to package it in a way that people are able to experience it in smaller pieces."

Under Wagner's direction, the SCCA recently launched its new Time Trial event. Time Trial is aimed at attracting beginners. One step above autocrossing, Time Trial offers a taste of competitive motorsports at a reasonable price point[68]. There are coaching sessions in the morning and other opportunities to learn and improve. Actual race time consists of multiple classes on track simultaneously based on qualifying times. Wagner is seeing a lot of interest and when the Time Trial schedule is announced the slots fill up quickly. To him it's proof that more people are interested in motorsports than ever before. They just needed traditional barriers to be torn down.

"To be relevant in today's culture we need to make significant changes," he told me. "There's a lot of people out there that don't want to be measured, scored—they just want a chance to drive their car in a fun, safe, legal environment. For us that's kind of uncharted territory. We're seeing a very different demographic: a lot more Millennials are active in that program; people with less time, income and knowledge about their car. And that's great. It's about trying to build a program around the idea that this is available to you."

The traditional strength of the SCCA, its racing, is under attack from another direction as well. One of the most popular racing series that has experienced huge interest and growth over the last decade is the 24 Hours of LeMons. Just like Radwood is a twist on the heritage of Goodwood, LeMons puts a mocking spin on the 24 Hours of Le Mans, perhaps the most prestigious motorsports event in the world. Just like Le Mans, LeMons races are about endurance and attrition. And just like Le Mans, LeMons features a wide variety of car classes and styles on track at the same time. That's about where the similarities end.

The endearing feature of LeMons is that the cars are supposed to be severely worn, torn and thrashed—lemons, basically. Participants are to enter cars that were purchased and race-prepped for a hard cap of $500. Five hundred. On a Le Mans car $500 might not be enough to replace an air intake. At LeMons it's the entire machine. Of course, this being racing, plenty of unsavory characters take the price limit as a challenge, a rule meant to be broken. There are always whispers and rumors about the actual price paid or who snuck what secret part by the judges. But for the most part people play by the rules. An intense scrutineering process and officials who often know the ins and outs of each car better than its owners make sure of that.

Part of the fun is in the decorations. Cars use elaborate modifications that make them look more like floats. They're crafted to look like forklifts, garbage collection trucks or a loaf of Wonder bread. One recreated "The Homer" from an episode of *The Simpsons*[69]. Giant figures of Snoopy, dragons and Marilyn Monroe ride on top of the roof. Most of the teams dress up.

While LeMons can be whimsical, the racing is real. All cars are fitted with approved roll cages and fire suppression systems—not counted toward the $500 cost. Drivers are required to wear neck braces and fire-retardant clothing[70]. The races last 24 hours and require multiple driver changes. Often there are on-spot mechanical challenges, making engine swaps, transmission replacements and other Herculean feats of engineering relatively commonplace in the pits.

It's a serious undertaking. In 2018 there were 21 races in the U.S., plus additional events in New Zealand and Australia. In addition LeMons held four 1,000-mile rallies and a car show called Concours d'LeMons, running concurrently with the Concours d'Elegance at Monterey Car Week. It's the kind of counter-culture celebration born of Internet-era irony that is like catnip to modern car enthusiasts.

LeMons is attracting people because of the affordability and the spectacle. But it also represents the branching out of motorsports. It's a response to demands that racing become more accessible and more fun; less uptight and bankruptcy-inducing.

In the LeMons vein there are competing events such as Chump Car and Lucky Dog Racing, fellow arbiters of the cheap and strange racecar. There is the Gambler 500, which takes any beater on four wheels and sets them loose in the Oregon wilderness. These series fit into the mold of taking bland, common and often exceptionally decrepit cars and going racing.

But when it comes to foolish racing in crappy cars there is nothing quite like the Broja 250. A play on the daunting Baja 500 and Baja 1,000 off-road races, Broja is one of a kind. Even compared to LeMons or Gambler it flies under the radar. There's no website, few photos and hardly any information online—unlike almost every event in today's era. Broja consists of a bunch of friends, mostly mechanics, who just want to take awful cars to the desert and beat each other up.

McQueen, the Driving While Awesome co-host and Radwood organizer, participated in 2017 with a beat up 1991 Ford Festiva nicknamed "The Blueberry." Against a field of two-wheel drive sedans and minivans with mismatched body panels and nonsensical rear wings, McQueen and his partner outfitted the Blueberry with Artrax tires meant for all-terrain turbocharged side-by-side vehicles. It won the off-road section and took fourth overall in the race that pitted eight terrible cars nose-to-tail against one another on makeshift courses that are rarely patrolled by law enforcement. The actual location of the race is closely guarded by organizers for obvious reasons. Cheating is encouraged. When a Ford Aerostar jumped the entire course of one portion in the desert and went from last to first it was called a "questionable move" and allowed to continue. Broja is to LeMons what LeMons is to the Indy 500. For the second run in 2018 participants outside of the original group of friends were allowed to enter. The number of entries increased from eight to 14. The cars kicked things off right by crashing into one another in the parking lot the night before the course pre-run[71]. The actual race was still weeks away.

If events like these are the future of car culture, we're in good hands. Depending on the event, attendance is up and down at car shows and motorsports events across the country, but hands-on participation and engagement is up. New kinds of experiences are sprouting that offer broader acceptance and wider appreciation. There are micro-niche events that celebrate specific styles and defined eras, even a certain type of engine style from one specific brand. There are competitions, mockeries of competitions and mockeries of the very idea of a sanctioned competition with rules and restrictions and even course boundaries. There is more variety than ever; and it's only possible because there are more dedicated car enthusiasts than ever.

In early 2018 I began to catch wind of pop-up car shows, a style I hadn't heard of before. I learned about it on Instagram, of course. The idea is modeled off the pop-up shop, a staple in the fashion and food industries when a brand holds a temporary storefront with limited supply. The show is called AutoConduct and its founder Ezekiel Wheeler, an experienced automotive journalist and communications specialist, organizes each at rotating locations in L.A. that are announced just days ahead of time. The cars that show up are often strange, even objectively bad—a perfect collection of Los Angeles style and impulsiveness.

I learned of the location on Saturday morning, loaded up my four-year old daughter, Claire, and headed to Alana's Coffee Roasters in Mar Vista, a small, hip neighborhood nudged up against Santa Monica. When we arrived, the parking lot was sparse but with no shortage of character. A gaggle of Porsches, a Plymouth Prowler, a Renault Fuego Turbo, Bryan Nigos' Rallyata, and a bright yellow 1978 Oldsmobile Ninety Eight with a rooster head and tail towering five feet out of the roof and trunk. Predictably, Claire loved the chicken car.

I found Wheeler at the food truck. He was speaking with Tommy Kendall, the championship driver of Dodge Vipers in the 1990s and the owner of "El Gallo," or The Rooster. Over the course of the night Wheeler would also welcome collection pieces like an olive green Lamborghini Espada and a gunmetal grey Peugeot 205 GTi. He would help the owner of a pristine Jaguar XJ220 supercar find a spot in the crowded lot and still find time to pass from car to car thanking everyone for coming. I thanked Wheeler for putting the show together and commended him for throwing a collection of people and cars that could only happen in Los Angeles. We didn't have much more time to talk. He had people to thank. And I had a tug on my shirt to go see the chicken car one more time.

Chapter VIII: Changing Faces

Ask the average American to conjure up their most accurate image of a "car guy" and they will likely have outdated ideas. It might be a teenager with greased hair in a muscle car; an engineer deep into the engine bay of an open-wheel racer at Indianapolis; or the aging owner of a Hawaiian button-up car shirt riding in a gleaming convertible with a baseball cap to cover a growing bald spot. Either way, it's likely a man. And he's likely white.

For many people, the idea of mainstream diversity in car culture began and ended with Danica Patrick. When, in 2005, Patrick became the first woman to lead the Indianapolis 500 and nearly won the most prestigious race in U.S. motorsports, she started a phenomenon that extended beyond racing. In many ways it extended beyond sports. At 23 she was a megastar. She would later become the first woman to win an Indycar race in 2008, and after switching to NASCAR, became the first to finish the Daytona 500—among many other milestones.

The story of her career should go down as one of the most impactful in U.S. racing history. To many it will be one of missed opportunity. Though Patrick proved herself capable of racing with the world's top drivers in multiple disciplines, something only a handful of racers regardless of background have matched, she never reached the lofty heights that others set for her. The 2008 win would be the only one in her career.

To the general public, Patrick's career is at best misunderstood. At worst, deliberate attempts to undermine her abilities and accomplishments have diminished what should be a monumental legacy. Patrick had to deal with accusations that her novelty, not her talent, kept her racing. It's true that her marketability elevated her profile and value to her team. But Patrick was, first and foremost, a damn good driver. Period.

The lack of full-time women drivers in Indycar and NASCAR that followed her is considered another knock on whether Patrick inspired young girls to enter motorsports. But teams and organizers must share responsibility for missing the opportunity to find and build careers for other talented women during her wave. There is evidence that Patrick's missteps were watched closely in order to justify higher-ups' inaction. And many believe that tide is changing now.

The reality is that, despite pervading challenges, women are finding their way in car culture in more ways and larger numbers than ever before. On the racing side they are engineers, race directors and of course drivers. On the enthusiast side they are collectors, rally organizers and club members. Fuel The Female, a non-profit organization that provides scholarships and networking opportunities for women in racing, highlights full-time mechanics, engineers, race directors, tire changers, event promoters, communications directors and more roles that women have found in motorsports recently.

"The sport will grow if we have more women in the sport," said Lyn St. James, an accomplished racer in open-wheel and sports cars, and behind the scenes advocate for women in racing. In 1992 St. James became the first woman to win Indy 500 Rookie of the Year when, at 45 years old, she finished in 11th place in her Indy debut. She holds wins at the 24 Hours of Daytona and Sebring as well as strong finishes at Le Mans and the Nürburgring. To many in the racing community, St. James is a household name. But she's one of many women who deserve better recognition from the general public.

Now retired, St. James runs the Project Podium development program for young women trying to make their way into a racing career. Through the program, St. James has mentored Patrick, Indy 500 veteran Sarah Fisher, Fuel The Female founder Katie Hargitt and hundreds of other women and girls. In racing circles, St. James is one of the most respected figures not only for her on-track commitment and success but her mentorship role in shaping the future.

"I never wanted anybody to think my reason for racing was just to prove women can do it—that was never my motivating factor. In reality I'm proud to say I did do that, I realize that now," St. James told me.

St. James had raced for decades by the time she came to a national stage in the '90s. Drivers and fans were aware of her abilities and welcomed her to the sport. But motorsport has not always been friendly to women. Despite a strong reputation, St. James dealt with sexism during her career, and even before it began. The first time she attended the Indy 500 as a young girl, women were not permitted to enter the pit area. The rule didn't change until 1974[72]. St. James cut a hole in the fence to watch teams roll their cars into the garages and prepare for the race. Decades later she would be welcoming women of all ages into her garage to sign autographs and show them around a 200-mph racecar.

"For two decades I was racing somewhere in a pretty visible, supported way. That left a dent. The part I couldn't control was getting the next wave to show up. Even though I couldn't control that, what I did do was create my development program to try and make a difference for those young drivers."

St. James fought and clawed her way through a motorsports career that started at age 27, much later in life than most. She started racing her own cars, finagled a sponsorship with Ford that lasted more than a decade and then entered the world of Indy ovals. In interviews, in her 2001 book "An Incredible Story" and in conversations with me, St. James detailed how her persistence and determination earned respect from her peers that has eluded other women drivers. That isn't to say that other women didn't deserve it, or that the road for St. James was carefree. She has told worrying stories about a team owner early in her career that demanded sex to keep her in the car, and how her refusal led to her exit, as well as the actions of another professional driver that in today's climate could have easily landed him in #MeToo hot water.

Blindness to the struggles women faced in automotive industries didn't stop once St. James graduated to management and advisory roles. A former member of NASCAR's advisory board, St. James recalled one meeting early in the 2000s. Executives were concerned that the sport's competitors are overwhelmingly white. In order to diversify its talent pool and potentially draw new fans to the sport, NASCAR has repeatedly aimed to attract drivers from different cultural backgrounds. The meeting that day focused on ways to attract Black and Latino drivers to stock car racing, including outreach efforts that would eventually lead to the series' founding its Drive For Diversity program in 2004[73].

"I'm listening to all this and I finally raised my hand and said, 'There's a population I know with a lot of talent out there, and that's women,'' St. James told me. "One of the biggest shocks I had, and this is still an issue today, is their concern was that it would be almost a turn-off if a woman went out there and beat the guys. They wondered, if Danica beat Jeff Gordon were they going to lose fans of Jeff Gordon? I'm like, 'Holy shit, you've got to be kidding me.'"

Danica Patrick never stormed the field in a way that challenged the male-dominated structure of NASCAR. While her presence in the sport marked a historically significant touchpoint, it hasn't led to the flood of other women drivers that some expected. The hesitancy among higher-ups in the sport as described by St. James could be a clue to the reasons why despite a deep and rich collection of women drivers across the country no team has been eager to put one in their car and give them a chance to compete. Opportunities for girls and women to learn and develop their skills on the track have grown exponentially over the last few decades, and by all accounts there is a welcoming and encouraging spirit at the grassroots levels for women looking to start a racing career. However, at the highest levels of competition, there are still larger patriarchal forces at play.

"There's only so many jobs right now," St. James said. "A lot of the leaders who happen to be men are not going to be too crazy about getting women into the sport because there is a concern they're going to lose their job to a woman. Nobody wants to lose what they already have. And that's cultural, that is not just in racing. Their idea is: we would love to have new talent, but we've got to worry about losing what we have."

To be fair, the boardroom conversation described by St. James occurred nearly 20 years ago. NASCAR has become markedly more progressive since then. Following the retirement of Patrick in 2018, the series welcomed the largest class of its Diversity Internship Program[74] which recruits women and students of color to earn hands-on experience, not only as drivers but a wide range of industry positions. Several alumni have graduated to full-time careers in NASCAR. The 18-year old driver Hailie Deegan is a full-time competitor in the K&N Pro Series West[75], a feeder minor league for budding stock car racers. In 2018 she became the first woman to win a race in the series. Many believe she's next in line for a full-time professional ride.

But that's currently the extent of prospective Patrick successors in stock cars. NASCAR has some women drivers competing in support series around the world but none threatening to enter the top-level Monster Energy NASCAR Cup Series. Patrick is the only woman to hold a full-time sponsored permanent ride and likely will remain so unless NASCAR gets serious about attracting and fostering female talent.

*

In 2017, the Formula One test driver Carmen Jorda drew headlines when she suggested the FIA create a separate racing series for women, giving them an opportunity to race against one another at a high level. To many, the plan was a sensible solution to a very real problem. F1 is extremely difficult to break into; each year only 18 spots are available. The ones that are not already taken by world champions, proven commodities and high-investment phenoms are offered to drivers that can bring tens of millions of sponsorship dollars along with them. Being a generational talent or being backed by corporate checkbooks are the only ways in.

F1 teams have hired women test drivers like Jorda, as well as mechanics and race engineers. Five women have attempted to compete in a Grand Prix; only two have ever qualified and raced. Italian driver Lella Lombardi holds the record for most races by a woman with 12 from 1974-76—she also scored a half-point in the 1975 Spanish Grand Prix[76]. No woman has ever won a Formula One race. So why not create a separate series for them to perform?

Jorda's full comments, however, were more direct. "It's not fair to be compared with men because we will never be on the same level," Jorda told the European network CSM Europe[77]. She later took to Twitter to clarify: "I believe a women's F1 championship would give us the chance to achieve our dreams and compete on an equal footing - as in other sports," Jorda said[78].

Not every female driver agreed. "Might help if we stopped giving weight to the opinion of someone who has less top ten results than Elmo from the Muppets..." tweeted Pippa Mann, an accomplished and respected open-wheel driver[79]. Mann also pointed out many women were currently rebutting Jorda's argument by not only hanging with the men, but beating them. Christina Nielsen had only weeks earlier been crowned champion of her class in the International Motor Sports Association, or IMSA, for the second consecutive season. Tatiana Calderon is the latest test driver for Alfa Romeo Sauber F1[80] and British driver Jamie Chadwick is widely regarded as most likely to follow in Lombardi's footsteps and compete in F1 races before long. Mann has written extensively about the issue on her personal blog, and pointed out the many successes of women racers and others as a rebuttal to Jorda's all-women's idea.

"This stripping of power away from female athletes, in one of the few sports where men and women can and do compete equally, was being presented as a way to empower us?" she wrote. "No thank you.[81]"

Despite Mann's perspective, Jorda's suggestion ultimately appeared to win out. The W Series, an all-women's open-wheel racing league, announced its first grid lineup in early 2019 and launched its inaugural race in May. Drivers from around the world were selected to compete with full team backing, including several well-known racers from the U.S. like Shea Holbrook and Sabré Cook—both of whom listed Lyn St. James as their racing hero[82]. Once the W Series got up and running, even those who agreed with Mann—who called the creation of the W Series "a sad day for motorsport"—initially seemed to lend their support to the league and its mission. Women deserve the chance to earn spots at the highest level. Race fans are hoping the W

Series spotlights the talent available and opens doors for drivers who were once fenced off.

*

While women continue to make headway in racing, in greater car culture female enthusiasts are a burgeoning community, growing in influence and number seemingly by the day. Just as the Internet and social media has allowed groups of niche fans to come together, it has done the same for highlighting women. Accounts like @FuelTheFemale on Twitter and @LadyDrivenAmerica on Instagram highlight dozens of women from greasy mechanics to budding racers. It's easier to find examples of female enthusiasts than any other automotive demographic on the Internet.

Even the SCCA, traditionally catering only to an insular community of hardcore racers—who are overwhelmingly male—is broadening its events in an effort to accommodate the growing number of women drivers in its ranks.

"We're more focused on the social development of driving rather than hardcore competition," Wagner, the SCCA organizer, told me. The two biggest reasons that newcomers, including women, are intimidated from participating in SCCA are time and money. The group is attempting to make events more accessible and affordable.

"We're trying to answer all those questions up front and work on letting people know this is something they can do. You don't have to be part of some secret organization."

The organization has an initiative called Women On Track[83] which works to promote the inclusion of women in SCCA events. Crucially, one of its stated missions is to break down traditional barriers that keep women from participating. There are scholarships doled out by a committee of experienced women drivers to cover costs and skirt entry fees. Wagner also pointed to regional off-shoots, like the active Facebook group Philadelphia Region Women on Track[84], popping up across the country.

On a sunny Saturday in February 2018 I met up with one prominent member of the growing women's enthusiast movement at Willow Springs International Raceway in Rosamond, Calif. Brionna Lynch, 21, is a professional Hollywood stunt driver. Her credits include *Creed*, *Venom*, *Black Panther* and filling in for Taraji P. Henson behind the wheel of a Maserati in the bullet-ridden film *Proud Mary*. Lynch is also a hell of a drifter. I met her on "The Balcony," a large section of asphalt hidden behind the main track grandstands where drivers congregate to share tips, work on their cars and toss themselves sideways at 80 mph inches from the concrete barriers.

When I arrive, Lynch is prepping her maroon Nissan 350Z for another smoky run. Her boyfriend, Nick Franco, lends a hand. They've already been here for hours and the stress of drifting is taking its toll on the cars, so maintenance is necessary if they want to keep running. It's a hot winter day with the sun pounding the asphalt and desert landscape around us. Worse is the wind, an unrelenting stream of whipping power kicked up from hundreds of miles away, hurling dirt and dust with it. When the cars drift by the wind carries marble-sized balls of rubber from the tires and sends them barreling into the face of anyone standing near.

These are less than ideal conditions for spectators, but to the drivers it's neither here nor there. Drifting is controlled chaos. A little crappy weather hardly registers. Lynch tightens the final screw and jumps into the Z. At 5-foot-0, she can barely see over the window sill—she and Franco had to move up the brackets to raise the seat so she could see out.

The cars go out four at a time. Lynch pulls into her place in line with the rest of her group. The field is heavy with Nissans, mostly the drift legend 240 SX, as well as another 350Z. There are several Miatas and even a Mustang in the mix. Compared with the rest of the field, Lynch's Z is understated. It still looks relatively stock and the sound from the exhaust note is high-strung and tinny rather than the chaotic booms, pops and rattles coming from the others. Many are literally falling apart, with recently-crashed body panels held together with zip-ties or tape. One has its roof sheered off. Another has ill-fitting bumpers and many don't have bumpers at all.

Lynch makes her way to the front and seems out of sorts. She takes the lead in her pack but spins on the first turn. The run is called off and the group returns to the line, again with Lynch in the lead. She swings through the first turn but spins on the second.

I'm standing on the sidelines next to Lynch's father, Jay, also a stunt driver who's worked on a litany of films including several in the *Fast & the Furious* series. When Lynch spins the second time he jumps on the radio and hollers instructions to heat up the tires. As her car comes around to file back into line Jay is screaming over the airwaves. "Start here and do a *manji* all the way down or do a fuckin' standing burnout!"

Lynch doesn't respond but the message is received. While the cars sit in line awaiting the next turn, she pulls into an open area and performs a series of donuts, smoky pirouettes that clear her mind from the previous runs and heat up her tires for better grip. On the next run she skates flawlessly through the first two turns, takes an aggressive line around the electrical box and leads the pack through the largest sweeper in full opposite lock. A friend sitting shotgun in Nick's car aims his camera at Lynch as both cars swing around, side-by-side, inches away from each other and the wall. Lynch and the friend could have reached out their windows and high-fived. All four cars blast out of the final turn to finish a perfect run. They re-enter the line and do it again.

Jay nods and turns to me. "That's what I'm talking about," he says. "I'm not trying to give her a hard time. I'm trying to help her solve problems."

Lynch returns to the lot to cool down the car. She watches a few runs, then takes Jay's girlfriend Tiffany out for a ride. Lynch and her father are close, sharing the house where she grew up in the L.A. suburb of Northridge. The running joke is that the two can share space, but their cars can't. The backyard is paved over with a jellybean-shaped pool in the center, and cars are constantly arranged around its perimeter in various states of repair. There's Lynch's Mini and her Nissan, Jay's black Corvette, two Mustangs and a Hummer H2. And occasionally Franco's BMW.

Weeks after our meeting at The Balcony, Lynch buys a newer blue 350Z that's intended to be an upgraded drift project. Instead, it's a comedy of car builds. The Z spends months disassembled next to the pool as Lynch and Franco take it apart and put it back together again. Over the course of several months the duo will build roll cages, replace dozens of components, install new engines, blow them up and re-install new ones. Lynch once posted a clip of Jay behind the wheel of her blue Z, burning out in front of their own house and abruptly slamming on the brakes. What he didn't realize was the hood wasn't screwed on. When the car stopped the hood flew off the front and crashed to the ground to howling laughter from them both. "He claims he's a 'professional stunt driver…'" read Lynch's caption.

Drifting and wrenching is more than a passion. For Lynch it's only the beginning. She sees a long-term career in cars. Lynch will continue honing her skills and hopes to expand her stunt work into more film and television. She launched a YouTube channel called Max-E Factory that features videos of the builds, racing and teammates in action. In a do-it-yourself world, Lynch is learning to build an audience that could lead to future opportunities. And she's finding a public that is more than receptive to what she's doing.

Lynch is a friend and frequent collaborator with Emelia Hartford, the drifter and YouTube personality. The two share a lot in common, from taste in cars to vlogging styles. One thing that Hartford is experiencing now, and Lynch is beginning to see, is prejudice baked into some of the feedback that comes her way. Hartford told me about it when we met at the 2018 Japanese Classic Car Show along the Long Beach waterfront. Hartford wore a black Period Correct baseball cap for shade from the September sun. She joked with my daughter and thanked a fan who gushed and said she loves Hartford's videos.

"It was always weird to me when women would tell me I'm am inspiration. For the longest time I just didn't understand it," she said. "In my mind, if I can do it then you can too. But I'm realizing it's unique to me and I'm still trying to understand it, to be honest."

Hartford is an effusive personality on screen, but here at the show, discussing her place in automotive culture, she seems stuck in the middle. Too often, Hartford told me, she has to explain how a woman like her could be into cars. When she includes other women in her content Hartford feels the need to over-vouch for their credentials, a preemptive strike against the backlash she imagines male viewers will send her way. Hartford still gets ignored by men at car events but insists that she feels that part of the culture is fading.

"I don't want to be treated differently because I'm a girl," she said. "But I feel like, if anything, we have a different standard."

Though we are still decades away from equity in motorsports, and much more needs to be done to increase diversity among both drivers and fans, the reality is that the car guy, and our consensus idea of what a car guy is and represents, is dead. There will always be men cruising in Corvettes, polishing their classic American iron and turning wrenches in their garage. There will always be teenage boys comparing rims and wings in grocery store parking lots. But women and people of color are a growing group within this community. And the community should be labeled automotive enthusiasts, a more inclusive term reflective of its members.

Automotive enthusiasts includes seasoned racecar drivers like Lyn St. James. It includes race directors like Leena Gade, engineers like 2018 IndyCar champions Kate Gundlach and Danielle Shepherd. It includes rally organizers and social media personalities like Aimee Shackleford. And it includes Brionna Lynch, swapping engines in her crowded backyard between stunt doubling for A-list actresses and whipping up tire smoke at drifting sessions. Maybe one day it will include my daughter, who said goodbye to Hartford and gave her a high-five. We headed off to see the rest of the show. She felt particularly drawn to a Toyota Van with a motorcycle mounted inside, a Honda Vamos with plaid cloth seats and a Hello Kitty-themed Mazda RX-8. Good choices all. She asked to watch Hartford's videos when we got home.

The car guy is dead. Long live the auto enthusiast.

Chapter IX: Supercars for the Masses

The booming voice of iconic racing commentator John Hindhaugh came floating over the telecast, as it had hundreds of times before.

"Here we are at Silverstone, home of the British Grand Prix," Hindhaugh said. As he spoke, a snaking field of high-powered Dodge Viper ACRs took off at the start and barreled into Turn 1. Each word out of Hindhaugh's mouth grew more excited.

"It's a decent start right at the front, already challenging for position as they make their way through."

The field bumped and blasted their way down the track, each one decorated in elaborate paint schemes showing off their teams and hinting at the scintillating performance lying underneath. Hindhaugh, with a trademark authoritative tone punctuated by an eastern UK accent, provided illuminating insight as the race progressed as if he were floating overhead, and watching the action unfold from above.

"Three-wide towards the end! This is awesome stuff."

Hindhaugh has been present for nearly all of the top sports car races for the past 30 years. But for the Viper race at Silverstone, he wasn't at the track. In fact, no one was. The racers themselves weren't there. They weren't even in the same room. Instead the competitors were all at home, racing virtually from their bedrooms and basements over the video game Forza Motorsport 7. Hindhaugh commentated live as he watched from a studio in Seattle.

"It's going to be a drag race to the line! It's going to be close here guys if there's any mistake on the exit! Here comes Laige! He is going to take 12 points here surely as he dashes to the line. And he does take it! Wow!"

Twelve of the top racing gamers in the world tore across the finish line to bring the action to a close. It was the first of three races in the Wednesday Showdown, an exhibition event streamed live over the Internet to drum up interest in the Forza Racing Championship, an open professional tournament that would run through the summer. With slots available by invitation only, the competitors battled for hundreds of thousands in prize money.

Racing video games are big business. The presence of Playstation and Xbox consoles has become ubiquitous across U.S. homes and cars play an outsized role in the industry. Along with the rise of the Internet, which gave birth to forums, blogs and social media apps as places to discover and absorb oneself in automotive content, video games are introducing and connecting people to car culture in new and lasting ways.

Forza, though it's available only on Xbox, is one of the most successful franchises on any genre in video game history. Likewise, its Playstation counterpart, Gran Turismo, is an icon of gaming in general. Together, along with a wide range of competitors, they brought a wave of enthusiasm to e-racing and inspired an entire generation of car enthusiasts in the process.

Now, some are attempting to transition virtual racing into real-life motorsports. ForzaRC marked its third season in 2018 with two knockout-style tournaments during the summer, culminating with an ultimate championship in October. The top racers in the world were invited to Seattle, then Mexico City and finally London for a chance to compete for the top spot. The addition of Hindhaugh was intended to draw audiences that would turn e-racing into a spectator sport on YouTube, Twitch and other gaming stream sites.

The tactic works for other games: the juggernaut shooters *Fortnite* and *Overwatch* regularly attract millions of viewers for the largest competitions with enough prize money to change any teenager's life.

In car-racing games, there are other perks. Competitors in the F1 2018 game have the opportunity to be "drafted" by real racing teams that now field official entries in the F1 Esports Series. Two-time F1 champion Fernando

Alonso formed his own virtual team with a consortium of gaming companies, called FA Racing G2 Logitech G, that signs bedroom drivers to compete across a range of games and platforms. Other games such as Forza, F1 2017, iRacing, DiRT, NASCAR PEAK and more combined to form a leaderboard that awards points and ranks the world's top 50 video game drivers according to their success across the board[85].

"It's been partly for us to spot who the best guys are out there," Joseph Barron told me. Barron is the marketing director for Slightly Mad Studios, which produces games such as *Project Cars 2* and *Need For Speed*. "The leaderboard creates opportunities for scouting as well: you can find an up and coming guy and offer them a more permanent deal."

Newer games like *Forza*, *F1* and *Project Cars* are determined to grow audiences and legitimize their e-sport as true racing, but when it comes to gaming prestige though, *Gran Turismo* is unparalleled. When Polys Entertainment, now Polyphony Digital, first released *Gran Turismo* for the Sony Playstation in 1997, it launched the idea of a story-style racing game that awarded points and newer, better cars as you won races and rose through the ranks. It brought a variety of cars that could be modified for better performance. It offered original tracks with unique style and then-stunning graphics, plus handling dynamics that felt less cartoonish than other games at the time. It felt more like you were behind the wheel of a real racecar. Winning a race against your friends became less about crashing them out and more about using skill and guile to outmaneuver them. Many credit Gran Turismo with giving real-world rise to the legend of the Nissan Skyline GT-R, a model that was at that point unknown in the U.S., even to enthusiasts.

In 2008, the game's developer, Polyphony Digital, partnered with Nissan to create the GT Academy—a tournament-style driving competition to whittle the best gamers in the world down to a single champion. The winner earned a chance to start a true professional driving career. In the decade since, GT Academy has gone through multiple iterations and produced several winners who have seen success on both the virtual and actual racetrack.

In 2011, three years after he became the first GT Academy winner, Spanish-born Lucas Ordóñez stood atop the podium at the 24 Hours of Le Mans with a second-place finish in the P2 class[86].

"Never in my wildest dreams did I think that [GT Academy] would take me all the way to the Le Mans podium," Ordonez said at the time. ForzaRC gives you the chance to be in a game announced by John Hindbaugh; GT Academy gives you the chance to be in an actual race announced by John Hindbaugh—and hold up a trophy at the end.

There have been others that used video games to launch real-life racing careers. Tommy Gorman, a full-time racecar driver for Honda in the Pirelli World Challenge, cut his teeth on video games as a child and continued using them for practice after his performances in autocross and amateur road racing took off. Bryan Heitkotter had only competed in autocross events when he won the GT Academy in 2011. He ended up racing several seasons in PWC and finished third in the overall standings in 2015.

In early 2019, the Italian gamer Enzo Bonito caught a lot of attention at the annual Race of Champions—a real-life, Olympics-style motorsports event that pits world class drivers head to head in a variety of racing disciplines to determine an overall winner. At the event in Mexico City, the 23-year-old Bonito took the wheel of a real car, lined up against former F1 driver and defending Formula E champion Luca di Grassi. And smoked him. On the second day of competition, Bonito beat Indy 500 winner Ryan Hunter-Reay[87]. On paper, it looked like an incredible mismatch—video gamer takes down two champion drivers—and an even more incredible upset.

But Bonito is more of a ringer than he may appear. The Italian is a full-time member of the McLaren Shadow Project, the official e-sports racing team under the legendary F1 team. Bonito also won the 2018 eROC, a virtual tournament, and finished 12th overall in the 2018 F1 Esports Series[88]. He was already a well-known talent in the gaming world. But with those eye-catching victories, Bonito is on the radar of real teams to pilot real cars. And earn real money.

*

This is a unique opportunity that racing games offer competitors. Winning tournaments in Call of Duty doesn't make you a good soldier. Beating Super Mario Bros. doesn't make you a plumber. The same goes for sports: the top e-sports players in basketball, football or soccer games would never last a minute against professional athletes. Can you imagine applying this to boxing? But racing gamers can translate their skills to the track as professionals. There are physical requirements, training adjustments and other nuances. But it can, and has, been done.

"What's interesting to me is going back to the Jim Clark era in the early '60s," Wagner, the SCCA organizer, told me. "You had guys that were farmers and went to the track and were fast and got pulled up because of their talent. As becoming a racecar driver became something that was internationally desirable I think the access first went to families that could afford it."

"In the past, families put aspiring drivers in situations to be seen so they could get their break—and in some cases, buy that break. Now with video games, people can develop that skillset affordably for the first time in half a century. And when given a chance they can perform at a high level in a racecar. It's a huge game change."

Playstation and Nissan say that about 400,000 gamers enter the GT Academy competition for their chance at racing stardom each year[89]. *Forza Motorsport* lists more than 2,100 drivers on its global rankings and the top 623 in North America[90]. More than 35,000 gamers have actively competed in *Project Cars 2* e-gaming, according to Barron.

"Of those, probably 4,000 we would consider in that tier where they're semi-professional in ability level," he said.

Millennials and post-Millennials are driving this revolution in gaming. *Project Cars 2* also has more than 166,000 fans on Facebook and 50,000 followers on the streaming platform Twitch. *Forza Motorsport 7* has more than 533,000 fans on Facebook and 220,000 on Twitch. All of the 18 drivers selected for

ForzaRC's 2018 tournament were young. One driver[91], at 24 years old, referred to himself as "a senior citizen." (One thing the gaming world does notoriously lack is diversity—no women were selected for the ForzaRC tournament and the only drivers who could be considered non-white were from Brazil and China. One each.)

The connection between the worlds of virtual and real motorsport is growing stronger, Barron said. Many gamers are trying to earn prize money to launch their own karting careers. That's why motorsports gaming needs two things to grow: increased participation from manufacturers; and increased prize money to allow the best drivers to hone their skills and fund a real racing career. The French car maker Renault recently sponsored the Renault Esports Series on *Project Cars 2* which offered a day of testing at its Palmer Sport track as the grand prize[92]. In 2017 the historic racing marque McLaren signed the winner of the World's Fastest Gamer eSports competition as an official simulator test driver[93].

"You'll see more things like that," Barron said. "There are a few soccer teams who have official FIFA gamers. But the skills aren't translatable, whereas the only thing a sim-racer doesn't have to deal with are the fear of pain and the fear of an expensive accident. The actual feedback is nearly one-to-one with a good wheel and set of pedals. The question is whether that makes it interesting for an audience to watch, or whether it's less attractive. Because if I'm watching someone do this in a game, shouldn't I just be watching the real thing? There's no data yet to say which way it will go."

E-racing is still in its infancy, and it seems there is room to grow. At the 2018 Special Olympics in Seattle, *Forza Motorsport 7* became the first video game to ever be included as an official event. Some wondered whether that could eventually open the door for video games to one day enter the Olympics themselves.

*

Part of the appeal for racing gamers is the thrills and excitement of driving fast that was once reserved for a select few. For less than $500 a gaming console and the latest racing title can offer players the experience of driving their dream car.

Video games have democratized the supercar, delivering access to the most exclusive driving experiences in the world from your couch or computer chair. Enthusiasts no longer have to pour over glossy magazines to memorize specs and download action-blurred photos to their brains. Instead you can turn on a screen, plop into a racecar, take a cruise in your tuner project, shoot for top speed on a test course, or measure yourself against real-world lap times on famous race tracks, just like in real life. Each car in the game handles differently, reacts to the changes you make, rewards your skills and punishes mistakes. Virtual or not, the feeling is immersive—and it's what enthusiasts have been chasing for generations.

In the final race of the ForzaRC Series 1 playoffs in 2018, the German gamer Robin Betka, known by his gamer tag b0x, crossed the finish line after a dramatic comeback that saw him crash on the first lap and drop into last place. He furiously worked back through the field to finish seventh, earning enough total championship points to win the top step on the podium and a check for $30,000 (presented to him by five-time X-Games gold medalist and rally driver Tanner Foust). As the commentators discussed the results, the camera continued to cut to b0x, still breathing hard in his simulator seat, wiping away tears[94].

"It's so good to finally have the payoff," he said in a post-race interview. "I didn't think this would ever be possible."

*

Where video games allow enthusiasts to embody and become a part of their love for racing, a similar phenomenon occurs on the Internet. Online forums help enthusiasts discuss and uncover stories outside of what they could read in magazines. Fan groups on Facebook, passionate accounts on Instagram and other social media platforms allow them to share and discover great cars that won't make it onto television. Beginning in the late 1990s, video games, online communities and social media started turning automotive enthusiasts from subscribers and viewers into participants and even influencers with audiences of their own.

The first transformative automotive experience I ever had, as many Millennials would agree, came from behind a video game controller. At 13 years old my friends and I piled into a buddy's house to try the hottest game, *Need For Speed III: Hot Pursuit*, an arcade-style racer that focused more on thrills than realistic gameplay. New for 1998, *NFS3* was addictive—it even let you run from the cops. I had already been a fan of Indycar and American muscle. While I wasn't obsessed or even particularly knowledgeable about cars, it was enough to deem me "the car guy" in our group. But sitting on the carpet in the SoCal den with a Playstation controller in hand, watching a Ferrari 550 Maranello come across the screen, everything changed.

I instantly committed that model name and its shape to memory. I don't remember whether I won or lost any races that night, but I'll never forget staring at the bright red 550 as it rotated on the tiny TV screen until my friends yelled at me to pick a car and start the race. I begged my parents to buy the game for me, and when they did, I raced the 550 incessantly. Sometimes I just drove around the game tracks, staring at the reflections dancing off the car's long front hood and aggressive side intakes. I thought it was the most beautiful thing I'd ever seen, and still feel that way. A few years later, the 550 I had discovered through a video game became my gateway to discovering the website Supercars.net, at the time the largest car forum community on the Internet.

By then, the car was five years old, and about to be replaced by a newer version. The magazines had stopped talking about the 550 Maranello and I'd worn out the VHS tapes with old television reviews I'd recorded. But on Supercars.net there were thousands of cars with their own individualized forums—basically personalized communities to talk about any model that had ever existed. The section for the 550 was rabid with action. Many of the posters seemed to have a lot of first-hand experience driving and owning exotic, high-priced supercars. It took me more than a year to realize that nearly all of them were just like me: passionate, car-crazy teenagers who stumbled from one argument to another, spreading ill-informed opinions across the site like shrapnel from a cluster bomb of inexperience. But that was part of the fun—finding your place, refining your interests, learning to vet sources and figure out how the car world works.

"In the mid-'90s the idea of journalism online was really cool," said Richard Owen, a classic car restorer and photographer. On a whim, Owen co-founded Supercars.net in 1999 as a place to document the car shows he attended and post thousands of his personal photos. He designed the site architecture himself and maintained it for more than 15 years.

"It was like having a magazine but there were no limits," Owen told me. "We'd go to Pebble Beach, Goodwood and other concours and we could just throw photos online."

Internet users jumped all over Supercars.net. Other automotive forums had existed before it, but the site became a general catch-all for enthusiasts and especially young people just getting started in car culture.

The general automotive forums were divided into categories: American, European, Asian, Classic, Motorsports, Design, etc. It was a great place to dive into what was going on in the car world at any given moment. Before blog-style car websites were posting by the minute, forum members threw up press photos of the just-released Lotus or Lexus within moments of the announcement—a practice that angered automakers at first. Several threatened to sue Owen and ban him from events, but they soon realized the inevitability of content being posted online.

At the height of Supercars.net, Owen could not keep up with the traffic demands on the site. He kept two servers at a remote site in Fremont, Calif.—one to handle web traffic and one to manage the forums. They were constantly crashing. "When you start getting that many requests it really loads up," he said.

And it never fully replaced the more traditional outlets. We were all reading *Road & Track* and watching *Top Gear*. It didn't discourage us from leaving the house and participating in car culture either—we shared updates on project cars, posted photos from car shows and wrote lengthy descriptions of our racing experiences. One user had the Supercars.net logo tattooed on his arm. During its heyday, Supercars.net members posted thousands of comments per day. It was in many respects, the precursor to modern automotive news websites.

"It was totally chaotic having that many people throwing around ideas and information," Owen said. He sold the site in 2016 to a vice president of the blogging platform Weebly. The new owners scrubbed Supercars.net of its forums and the millions of posts that accumulated over the years. My account still works but the activity is gone. Instead of the painstaking back end that Owen slaved over for years, the site is now hosted on Wordpress. But Owen's images, descriptions and event recaps still remain, and he harbors no hard feelings about the shift.

"I was Mr. Supercars.net for 15 years," he told me. "Everywhere I went people knew the website. But I'd just been doing it for so long. The whole thing was based on ad revenue and revenue was going down. If we were to continue the way we were going we would've been sunk. I was no way prepared to ever get that far. And besides, I like where it is right now."

Today, social media has largely replaced forums as cultural torch-bearer for budding young car enthusiasts. Facebook and Twitter are full of healthy communities engaging in lengthy debates. YouTube is an insatiable horde of auto nerds demanding lust-worthy slow motion shots of burning rubber and glistening carbon fiber. Forums are still around, especially brand-specific ones where owners can confer to share advice and war stories, but largely they've dwindled or, as Emelia Hartford put it to me, their users are "modernizing," aka, migrating to other platforms. Automotive content has come a long way since buff books and *Top Gear.*

*

Like forums were in the early 2000s, Instagram is the key driver of online car culture today. The mobile photo app is easy to navigate, encourages participation and fosters interaction. Most creators are far more likely to engage in discussion on Instagram than any other platform, meaning you can strike up a conversation with your favorite reviewer or engineer or even champion driver through the comments or direct messages without much delay. This makes fans a living and breathing part of the conversation—not simply observers. It also makes builders and creators of personal projects more likely to gain followings of their own.

When the Bridan brothers first began posting photos of their Dropped Alfa rally car project, they had no idea what to expect. "We thought we were going to get a lot more hate than we did," Iliya told me. "When it was all positive-positive-positive it was like, 'Huh, guess people kind of like this thing.'"

Early into the process one Saturday morning, the Bridans brought the Alfa to Cars & Coffee Trancas, a premier weekend car show in an exclusive oceanfront enclave in Malibu. The parking lot is regularly stuffed with priceless classics and sparkling new hypercars fresh from surrounding dealerships. The rules are clear: no touching, no loud burnouts. Essentially, no disheveled behavior. The Bridans pulled in with their loud, noisy, dirty Alfa rally car while it was still dark out before anyone could turn them away.

"The Trancas people didn't even look at it. Basically everyone ignored it," Iliya said.

"They were pretending they couldn't see it," Nikita said.

"It was invisible to them," Iliya said. "There was a Lexus LFA parked next to it and everyone was ignoring the Alfa. Maybe a month later it got pretty big on Instagram. Other designers from Europe in car studios started messaging me like, 'I love this car, this is my screen saver.' When you get the respect of your peers, you know you've done well."

Within weeks Dropped Alfa surpassed 5,000 followers. The Bridans were invited to appear in films and photo shoots. When the car collective Hoonigan invited the brothers to shoot a video they talked Iliya into jumping the Alfa off a ramp. It took the first leap with no problem, so they moved it farther back. Iliya hit the ramp harder, flying so far over the ramp the front underpinnings crashed straight onto the pavement. The oil pan shattered and fell off, the brakes wouldn't work and the car slammed into the chain link fence surrounding the shop. Dropped Alfa needed another rebuild. But within months the car was kicking up dust in the desert again. They're now over 10,000 followers.

"Being a car designer I already know all the cars, I've seen all the cars," Iliya said. "If you just show me an F40 I'm like, 'Who cares?' I guess we're spoiled in California, we've seen all these things. But give me an F40 with like a roof rack that goes skiing through snow and stuff, that becomes so cool. Static is boring now, isn't it?"

The Bridans aren't alone. What plays well on Instagram is stuff that's being used. Whether it's racecars ripping on the track, muscle cars burning rubber or anything kicking up dirt. The off-road scene has experienced a resurgence in recent years that is due at least in part to Instagram users who post glamorous pictures of their adventures. It's led to a boom in aftermarket sales of outdoor-focused equipment like beefy tires, lifted suspensions and exterior equipment from bike racks to rooftop tents. Even more lucrative for the industry is that newcomers are flocking to the outdoors for adventure—some companies are expanding their product lines to include affordable and accessible items that make it easy for beginners to get their foot in the door. A world once reserved for the most hardcore desert rats has now expanded to yuppies and urbanites thanks to a mobile app.

*

It isn't just trucks. When I met with Bryan Nigos, owner of the Rallyata, he fired off a litany of off-road adventures he'd experienced just in recent months. Among them was King of the Hammers, an ultra-extreme rock crawling race for trophy trucks just south of the Mojave Desert. In more than a decade of running through the sun-bleached valleys, Hammers has seen few Asian-Americans and fewer Mazda Miatas. But this is no superficial build. Rallyata has a skid plate, front bumper bar, lifted suspension and off-road tires. Nigos converted the trunk into a beetle wings-style compartment that flips open to hold a dual rear tire carrier that would make any rough and tumble Hammers veteran squeal with glee. They reveled in the sight of the Rallyata tearing through the dry lake beds, Nigos told me.

Lifted Miatas is one of those hyper-niche car communities that can only evolve and thrive on a minute-by-minute app in the palm of your hand. There are tail-whipping rally Miatas, zombie-proof mudslingers with snorkels, converted racecars with a hitch and a winch and basically every other combination of wild and dirty fun you can think of. A few years ago it would have taken months for members to even find each other through the pages of bi-monthly magazines. Now it takes seconds. And you're conversing and sharing ideas that turn into builds within days.

Millions of car photos and videos are posted to Instagram every day. Car videos continue to swamp YouTube and car racing games will only become more immersive and more enticing as participation continues to climb. Car culture is better for it. It gives enthusiasts a virtual entryway to the community, helps people find where they fit in and introduces them to new ideas and trends that may normally be outside of their comfort zone. It's even influenced the highest tier of auto echelons. "At Pebble Beach the cars are better now—and it's because of the Internet!" Owen told me.

Chapter X: On the Block

In December 2017 I picked up my dad at his home in the San Fernando Valley and drove down Ventura Boulevard, toward one of the last remaining agricultural bastions of Los Angeles. We turned into the quiet neighborhood of Tarzana,[95] with its neatly manicured lawns on tidy square lots nestled into the foothills of the Santa Monica Mountains. Each home fit neatly into its assigned space.

Except one. Before the homogeneous neighborhood with its compliant properties was designed in a clearly defined grid, it was a massive citrus grove. Some 15,000 acres were covered in orange trees. Few people lived in the area and the ones who did were most interested in staying out of the way of the rest of burgeoning Los Angeles. Tarzana was happy to keep a low profile. Suburban creep put an end to that. Developers built houses on top of the groves and nearly wiped citrus farming from the area. But Lindley Bothwell looked at the area and saw potential.

Bothwell bought one of the last remaining groves in Tarzana after graduating from college in 1926[96][97]. By 1998 it had grown to nearly 2,000 trees and the land expanded to 14 acres. Bothwell owned 33 other groves across the country and amassed a fortune. On the ranch he built several garages, barns, stables and a fully-operating train on a railroad system that encircled the grove because it had become too big for Bothwell to monitor on foot. The neighborhood that stands today simply built up around the ranch. If you look at the area in online maps you'll see hordes of tiny rectangles butted up against the enormous Bothwell property like bees swarming their queen.

Lindley Bothwell died in 1986[98][99], leaving his considerable estate to his family, who still live on the property and operate the grove. Among their inheritance was hundreds of cars, many of them odd, notable or historically significant. Over the years the collection has slowly thinned out through private sales. In early 2017 the family approached the auction house

Bonham's about hosting a mass sell-off of the cars on the ranch itself. The one-night event would offer a massive array of trains, trucks and cars, with one crown jewel: a 1914 Peugeot L45 Grand Prix two-seater. The car could be described as the father of modern performance. It was as if the missing link came up for sale. Its engine was the first to ever feature dual overhead camshafts—twin rotating spits at the top of the engine that allow the cylinders to pump more efficiently, revving the engine higher and creating more power[100]. Today, essentially all performance cars and racecars follow the dual overhead cam formula. Peugeot was the first company to perfect the technique and they did it with the L45 Grand Prix. There are two left in existence. Lindley Bothwell owned one. Bonham's estimated its value at $3 to $5 million.

That is how my father and I found ourselves on the Bothwell property. It isn't difficult to attend an auction like this. Anyone interested can purchase an event catalog—containing detailed information on all of the units up for sale, with colorful backgrounds and the expected sale price—for $100. That earns entry for two people.

They day of the auction was one of those unseasonally warm winter afternoons in Los Angeles. When we arrived, valet parking on the property had already filled up. I parked in front of a middle school down the block and we walked past tuxedoed guides into the show. Upon entry, we were greeted by a row of cars that would be on the block that night—a 1900 Clément-Panhard with a rear-mounted one-cylinder engine and a canary yellow '08 Mercedes-Simplex that Bothwell raced around Southern California[101], including in a rally on Catalina island[102]. A lineup of early open-wheel Indy cars with varying degrees of significance and success were housed inside an adjacent five-car garage. There were Depression-era paddy wagons, fire trucks and hearses. We walked past Bothwell's famed railroad and a custom-built 1926 Rolls Royce Silver Ghost pickup truck, out into the orange grove proper. The fruit burst forth from the branches like fragrant Christmas ornaments that stretched as far as the eye could see.

The railroad led around the trees to an array of barns near the back of the property. We turned a corner and I was shocked by the scene. Bonhams had turned a literal orange farm into a high-class affair. A cash bar was situated to our right and servers carried trays of hors d'ouvres, finger sandwiches and, surprisingly, bags of potato chips for sale. To the left sat a full auctioneers table with the head announcer seated at center and associates working the phones in a frenzy on either side. TV screens illustrating the car up for auction and the current bid hung above his shoulders, facing rows of fold-out chairs and table-tops lined along the orange trees. Not a seat was empty when we arrived. We squeezed past the sparkling blue paint of the Peugeot cradling sodas and leaned our elbows onto a table-top that someone appeared to have intentionally set up as deep into the branches of an orange tree as possible.

One by one the remnants of the Bothwell collection came up for sale. The Clément-Panhard sold for $60,500; the Rolls truck went for $159,500. Then, early in the evening, almost abruptly, it was time for the main event: the Peugeot Grand Prix. The bidding started at $1 million. It was war. Sales agents manning telephones flanked the auctioneer on the stage and spoke frantically into receivers, gesticulating wildly when they had a bite. Two million. Three million. Once in a while a paddle raised calmly from the crowd of onlookers. Four million. Flatscreen monitors overhead showed the numbers ticking off by the hundreds of thousands every couple of seconds. My dad and I turned to each other, nursing our virgin Coca-Colas, giggling at the scene unfolding in front of us. Five million. There goes the estimate. Six million. In-person bidders pretending to act disinterested at their cocktail tables began to cool off, but the phone bids kept coming. Seven million. The monitor tickers slowed to a crawl. The bidders tuckered out. I stared at the Peugeot at the foot of the auctioneer. The car seemed to bask in its moment—Going once!—its endless blue paint—Going twice!—reflecting orange trees across its bonnet—Sold!—for the final time. The dust settled. Bonhams banged the hammer at $7,260,000—about 3,000 times the $2,500 Bothwell paid for it 70 years earlier.

*

It's odd to stand next to a vehicle that's just been pegged with a value of more than $7 million. Without question it is a stunning machine: each piece of metal shines as if it were just forged at the factory; the bare aluminum and brass interior looks ready to race, the deep blue paint ends in a sensuous teardrop. I can confirm that your reflection looks better in millions of dollars of metal than it does in your bathroom mirror.

But at the end of the day, this is an automobile like any other. It has four wheels, an engine and a steering wheel, and it gets you from Point A to Point B. The rest is details. There were two other million-plus sales in the Bothwell collection that night—both 1908 Mercedes-Benz racers—and the Peugeot made them look like used car lot lemons.

The sales that night had real-world repercussions. The results, determined by the whims of billionaires and the fixers they entrusted with their car budgets, placed values not only on the cars that were sold, but also set standards in the classic car market that would determine the price of future cars that come to auction.

I wanted to know more about how the world of high-priced auto auctions operates, so I turned to Jakob Greisen, the 37-year old head of Bonhams US Motoring Department. Greisen was at the Bothwell Ranch that night, one of the dozen or so Bonhams reps working the phones and running around in devilishly sharp suits. He said that the current state of the white-hot market, resulting in the kind of stratospheric prices commanded by cars like the Peugeot, began around 2010. As the country continued to crawl back from the Great Recession, economic indicators finally began showing signs of improvement by the end of that year[103]. We now know that the results of that improvement largely made its way to the wealthiest families in the country, inflating the upper middle class and elite with discretionary income[104]. By 2015, this trickled into the collector car market, which had about tripled in value, Greisen said. "It really brought a lot of focus on it," he told me. "We saw prices that were unheard of."

More than the increase in valuation, the kinds of cars that collectors were after had changed drastically in the process. The influx of money armed a new class of relatively young, Internet-savvy buyers who came of age with different tastes than the collectors before them. The first segment that began to materialize was the air-cooled Porsches (that would eventually lead to the cult of Luftgekühlt). Buyers who grew up as teenagers in the 1970s and '80s, salivating over the dramatic fenders and orchestral sounds of the 930, 964 and 993 began scooping them up in large heaps[105]. Cars that were once torn apart without a second thought and dismissed by collectors became some of the most desired on the market.

Along with the Porsches, other cars from that era began to balloon in value. The BMW E30 M3 and Mercedes-Benz 190E Evo were suddenly hot. Cars that either competed in or were influenced by Group B rallying, long considered unsophisticated and ugly, shot up in price. The Ferrari F40 and Porsche 959, the original supercars, juiced up like power-hitting sluggers. The rising tide lifted all boats. Soon everything from the '70s and '80s became collectible. Before long, the going rate for a 1973 Porsche 2.7 RS had grown from $40,000 on the low end to several hundred thousand dollars in value. From 2004 to 2014, the average 2.7 RS increased in value by 669 percent and the Discovery Channel named it the best car in which to have invested over the past 10 years. By the time the inaugural Luft came about in 2014, a 2.7 RS sold at auction for $1.42 million[106].

"Every decade has their most important cars," Greisen said. "The ones generally appreciated by younger collectors. There's always that 'Let's find them before they become valuable' thing."

The original frenzy has mostly cooled. The 2.7 RS is still selling at healthy prices and cars from its era are highly desired. But many people who wanted one either have them now or opted out of the bidding wars. These days, buyers are becoming more discerning about their purchases, seeking out the highest quality examples or special editions that are set apart. Greisen believes there are three qualities to a car, regardless of era, that can make it truly stand out from the pack and send prices sky-rocketing: aesthetics, engineering and history.

Aesthetics: "Anything cool, badass, beautiful. Like French cars from 30's, racing cars that were amazing looking but not necessarily pretty."

Engineering: "It has to stand out. Like the 959—technically, it was over the top."

History: "If it had a cult following, or made its mark on the time. That's significant."

Catch all three, he says, and you've got lightning in a bottle. With these qualities in mind, it's easy to see how a car like the 1914 Peugeot separates itself from the pack. Its looks are undeniable, its dual overhead cams were pioneering and its motorsports legacy can still be seen in the racecars of today. It's also a one-off design. Add it all up and $7 million starts to look like a bargain. It's certainly not just another Ferrari in the collection.

And if you apply the same formula to modern classics like the E30 M3 or Porsche 959, there appears to be staying power in their values. Millennial collectors will only continue to enter the market. Greisen said that the typical Bonhams buyer is about 50 to 75 years old because of the steep price of entry in the world of high-class auctions. However, Millennials are actively participating, and in many cases driving, trends that determine which models are most popular.

"We do definitely see interest from a younger generation. They tend to like cars from a more modern era, that's where they normally start. While it's true that some of them ease into appreciating cars that were made decades before they were born, they probably start with something they remember from their childhood," Greisen said.

Bonhams has sold to collectors in their 30s, he said. In fact, Millennial participation is up at all levels of auctions. In general, the large houses realize that many of their usual top spenders are, frankly, getting up there in age. Sending out a catalogue and waiting for the big money to roll in is not going to attract new buyers to take their place. As a result auction houses have worked to attract Millennials and other young collectors and bring them into the fold.

One of the largest and most visible car auctions is Barrett-Jackson, which holds three large televised events each year. Traditionally its collections lean heavily on American chrome and muscle—think big fins, big engines and fat tires. Think: flames painted down the side. Occasionally a pristine car at Barrett-Jackson will hit the $1 million mark—there are always a couple that go for several hundred thousand—but the meat of Barrett-Jackson shows is in the $30,000-70,000 range, an easy entry point for new bidders to begin their collection habit. And it's resonating with younger buyers.

In 2016, the mid-scale auction house noted that half of the people in attendance at its Las Vegas event were attending a Barrett-Jackson show for the first time. The following year, in Scottsdale, one of Barrett-Jackson's signature events, 40 percent of the bidders—not attendees, but bidders—were first-timers[107]. Through the first three events of 2017, more than 200 people between the ages of 18-37 signed up as new buyers[108]. If you really want to blow Malcolm Gladwell's mind, tell him Barrett-Jackson reported buyers even younger than Millennials signed up in significant numbers at its Northeast Auction in Connecticut. Generation Z is already showing its influence, too.

Data shows they're not just signing up to the events, they're following through. The classic car insurance agency Hagerty Inc. is used to dealing with high-net-worth clients and priceless machines. Now, out of necessity, it's learning to work with younger clientele. Hagerty launched a mobile app, called "Insider," to provide live coverage of the Arizona auctions in early 2018[109]. Barrett-Jackson saw the trade winds blowing and has reduced its offerings of muscle cars and post-war iron to grow its collection of nostalgic '80s and '90s models. European exotics and Japanese JDM cars, once met with disgust at the U.S.-centric Barrett-Jackson, are now right at home there. It's not uncommon to see a pristine 1994 Toyota Supra with a giant rear wing come across the stage[110]. Since 2016, Hagerty has seen a 21 percent increase in insurance quotes from Millennial collectors[111].

Even when they're not the ones buying, Millennial tastes are driving the market in other ways. A modernized 1971 Chevrolet K5 Blazer SUV sold for a world record $220,000 at the 2017 Barrett-Jackson auction in Palm

Beach[112]. “Long thought to be less interested in vehicle ownership and driving, 81 percent of millennial drivers taking part in the nationwide survey said they like, love or are passionate about driving,” according to a 2018 survey by Hagerty[113]. That’s higher than Gen X, at 78 percent, and Baby Boomers, at 79 percent.

“As of the fourth quarter of 2017,” read one analysis from Hagerty[114], “Generation X and the millennials have matched the boomers and their elders, the so-called greatest generation, in terms of demand.” In fact, Millennials are buying collectible cars at a rate that outpaces the growth of Baby Boomers or Generation X. “We are already seeing the influence of 100-million-strong millennials, who are entering the hobby in greater numbers every day,” the Hagerty report said.

The rise of the Millennial collector has had a growing effect on car culture. Demand for obscure or underpriced cars across all brands—thanks to an Internet-fluent customer base—began to grow at a pace matching the feverish classic market. Instead of running from one online forum or auction to another to find the right car, enthusiasts needed one central online marketplace. And that’s how Bring A Trailer was born.

*

Bring A Trailer launched in 2007 as a website selling unloved or fix-it cars at a listed price[115]. But in 2014 the website started hosting consignment auctions. Having already built a passionate following and developing connections to bring hot ticket items across the virtual block, BAT auctions quickly became must-read material for automotive enthusiasts, especially young ones. If you were looking for an interesting or promising car to get your feet wet in collecting, BAT quickly replaced Craigslist and eBay Motors as the go-to website. At any given moment today, there are hundreds of live auctions going on at once, ranging across the automotive spectrum. The site played a key role in the rush for air-cooled Porsches, the likes of which would soon find their way to Joey Seely or Luftgekühlt, or both. Six “Safari” Porsche 911s and 29 E30 M3s were listed on BAT in 2018 alone. As of late 2018 the site had hosted more than 10,000 listings.

As with many influential websites, the real magic is in the commenting sections of the auctions. Over the years BAT has accrued a following that encompasses every corner of the automotive enthusiast world. There are experienced collectors sharing valuable experiences, educated mechanics and obsessionals with attention to obscure detail and straight fans of the brand or period. And then there are people who don't know as much as they think, people who want to know more and aren't afraid to chime in with questions, and just general shit-posters.

As its name implies, Bring A Trailer traffics in cars that you will likely prefer to trailer, either because they're precious or collectible, or need to trailer because they're not street legal. Or they are currently operationally-challenged. The comment section is a great place to suss that out. If you're looking at, say, a Nissan R32 Skyline GT-R, a revered but complicated and still mysterious car to many, you'll find the right questions to ask almost immediately.

Stock exhaust? (Not many still have it.) Does the AC work? (Repairs are a bitch.) Is the boost restrictor still in place? (Good indicator of whether it's been tuned to death.) Where was it imported to? (Never buy one from Florida.)

The answers from sellers can shift the direction of the auction in real-time. In many cases, it's the difference between a 1989 R32 going for $24,000[116] and a 1991 R32 going for $30,123[117] just two months later. Clean, unsullied examples of these unicorn cars and the passion they attract are what keep people coming back to BAT even if it means ignoring work for an hour or bringing their laptop to the bathroom. (Both are frequent admissions in the comments.)

As with anything on the Internet that grows in popularity, Bring A Trailer has come under attack by people who think it has gotten too big too fast. Often the site lists cars that are newer, more trendy or more expensive than its core fanbase would like. The number of million-dollar sales on the site has increased dramatically in recent years. In September 2018 BAT listed a

Ferrari LaFerrari with 95 miles that rocketed up to a $3.25 million bid. It did not meet the reserve, but it did attract comments—1,672 in just five days[118].

What really gets the *Traileratti* going, unsurprisingly, is slow cars fast. With a built-in dedicated fanbase that is growing more educated and more appreciative of classics all the time, Bring A Trailer is the perfect place for moths to find their flame—suped-up factory cars like the Renault R5 Turbo 2. Beginning in 1980, Renault produced less than 5,000 examples of this tiny hatchback in order to take it rally racing. Its boxy silhouette is less than inspiring. Frankly, if you don't know what you're looking at, you'd assume it's slow as hell. But the quirky mid-mounted engine packing 158 horsepower to a five-speed manual and fender flares that seem to stretch to the moon cemented its legendary status. Inarguably, the R5 checks all three of Greisen's value-holding boxes.

Bring A Trailer sold its first R5 in 2016 for $63,000. Then another for $73,000[119]. But by the end of 2018 a similar example went for $95,000. The higher performance Evolution models easily fetched more than $100k. "This car went from WTF to WANT over the past couple years for me," one commentor wrote. "And it's all your fault BaT."

A similar trend hit another rally-inspired hot hatch, the Lancia Delta Integrale. It has the same pedestrian roots as the R5, with exaggerated bodywork, a turbocharged engine and all-wheel drive. Racing versions won six straight rally titles. Street versions sell lower than the R5, likely due to less horsepower, less eye-catching design and more production numbers, but the passion surrounding the Integrale is just as feverish.

A chart graphing the car's sale results looks like the torque curve of a turbocharged engine—it shoots up over time with no signs of slowing down[120]. What started as a sub-$17,000 car took a year to grow to the $25,000 range and then blasted north to $70,000 by 2018.

The reason isn't simply that buyers started suddenly appreciating the car. Integrales have always been held in high regard by those in the know. What started happening is BAT gained a reputation and, in the process, pulled better cars out of the woodwork. In 2017 sellers started posting the highly-coveted Evolution models to the site. One missed its reserve at $38,000. Two sold in the $40,000 to 50,000 range. When a standard Integrale fetched $42,000 that seemed to accelerate things. Now Evos jumped from $53,000, to a missed reserve at $62,000 and then a sale at $70,000.

Near the end of 2018, Bring A Trailer hosted a meet-up for owners who purchased their vehicles from the site. Hundreds of cars showed up. The Petersen Museum hosted the event and it took over the entire top floor of its parking garage. Matt Farah was there. Children ran around with cameras at the ready. I spoke to two Croatian art students who now live in L.A. and came hoping to catch a glimpse of rare Porsches and Lancias. They got their wish.

Amid a sea of collector cars and cult classics, the primo spot, right in front of the BAT tent, was reserved for a Delta Integrale. When it arrived on the top level of the structure, rising from the ramp like a white whale summoned from the deep, Bring A Trailer founder Randy Nonnenburg sprinted to cut it off and direct the driver to the position. The owner parked and popped the rear engine bay, which requires lifting the entire back end of the car. If there were any S4 non-believers in that crowd, they are no longer. Nonnenburg is a man who understands his customers. He told me that BAT has changed based on tastes and trends. And more often than not those trends are determined by the youngest members of the *Traileratti*.

"Our audience skews younger because it's a technology platform," Nonnenburg said. "They're very comfortable seeing stuff on a small screen and our product appeals to that. The younger crowd has more trust buying online, they grew up on Amazon. But at the same time they expect a higher level of transparency. They didn't grow up doing handshake deals. If they want to see a picture of a part they expect to get it quickly. We align really well there, kind of through luck."

As we talked I looked around at the collection gathered in the lot. People laughed and joked over a rare Subaru SVX or a tiny Honda S600 with a motorcycle engine installed. A sterling E30 M3 sat next to an orange Lancia with rally lights and a racing stripe. An absolutely perfect silver Jaguar E-Type, an Outlaw Porsche Speedster and Bruce Meyer's yellow on black Type 57 Bugatti represented the traditional collector set. Two Renault R5 Turbos, one red and one blue, attracted crowds all morning. In the middle of our conversation a man approached Nonnenburg to say he's been selling BMWs for decades.

"It's gonna be BAT or nothing for us," he said. I asked Nonnenburg if he envisioned this when he started the company.

"No," he said. "All of this has been a wonderful surprise. We didn't even start the website with a business in mind. We didn't even start the listings with an auction in mind. It's all been pretty organic of what we found the market has needed and wanted. We've been lucky to be the ones to lead and fill that void."

*

Enthusiasm drummed up in part by BAT has spread beyond the Internet as well. In January 2018 the annual Bonham's Scottsdale auction offered a 1982 Lancia 037 Stradale, the road-going version of a rear-wheel drive rally car that competed in the unlimited Group B class. In an auction that included bona fide, 70-year-old classics from Ferrari, Porsche, Mercedes-Benz and Bentley the Lancia stuck out. Its final sale of $451,000 that launched it into the weekend's top ten results[121], surprising many. "It would have sold for $150,000 a few years ago," Greisen told me.

The Lancia was the only car in the top ten built in the 1980s. As a direct descendant of the Group B era, which is quickly gaining steam as the modern day equivalent of the 1960s golden age of racing, the 037 is a sterling example of the new wave of unloved cars turned inarguably collectible. Comparable boxy stars include the Audi Sport Quattro, Ford RS2000 Evolution and Lancia Delta S4—all routinely attracting estimate sale prices of a half-million dollars, according to Hagerty[122]. Baby brother members of the group like the Peugeot 205 Turbo and Renault R5 are now easily six figures. And it's at least in part because of young people discovering these cars that were built, raced and retired long before their birth, online.

"Recognition of their performance is helped in no small measure by copious YouTube videos of them jumping, sliding, weaving, and making handbrake turns in the hands of brave drivers with superhuman car control skills while navigating snow, ice, gravel, tarmac and desert sand. Spectators crowd onto the unprotected tracks, parting like waves as the cars come through on the ragged edge of control," Rick Carey wrote in Hagerty.

Because of the vast availability of information on the Internet, several people told me, buyers are more knowledgeable than ever. They're less reliant on the opinions of friends, family and car show attendees. They're more resourceful in finding documentation and determining a car's proper place in history.

In December, 2018 the auction house RM Sotheby's announced it had acquired a treasure trove of more than 140 Radwood-era vehicles from a single buyer[123], and would offer the entire collection across four events held around the world. The firm specifically highlighted notable cars such as the Porsche 928 and Renault R5 Turbo, and pointed to the rise in young Millennial collectors as a deciding factor in its acquisition.

"The '80s and '90s 'youngtimers' are back and here to stay in the world of car collecting, and we're thrilled to offer this extensive collection on behalf of its enthusiastic owner," said Gord Duff, the global head of auctions at RM Sotheby's. Two of the four events will be held in the U.S., specifically in Florida. Some of the biggest cars on offer include the Acura NSX and Toyota Supra, cars once sneered at by serious collectors and left to Japanese enthusiasts now command special attention at global events. The second Florida auction will even feature multiple Nissan 300 ZX, which RM Sotheby's called "an appreciating future collectible."

I spoke with Matthew Ivanhoe, founder of the Cultivated Collector private sales house and the owner who brought his zero-mile Schuppan 962 to Luftgekühlt. Ivanhoe started his brokerage business in 2017. Since then his main clientele has shifted in age from their 60s and 70s. Now the age of his average buyer is down to the late 40s.

"My client base has encountered a notable dip," Ivanhoe said. "It's due entirely to the fact I've seen a strong increase in the guys who are in their early 30s who've started to make a little bit of money and are starting to buy cars. Which is exactly how it all gets started."

The cars offered at Cultivated Collector are not for beginners. Ivanhoe's sold vehicles include concours winners like a 1937 BMW 328, historical landmarks like a 1956 Ferrari 250 Europe GT and true rarities like a 1991 Jaguar XJR15[124]. One lineup for sale included a 1962 Aston Martin DB4 suggested at $444,000[125], a 1961 Lancia Appia Sport Zagato for $215,000[126] and a 1987 Sierra RS Cosworth—a rally-inspired cousin of the Group B descendants—for $60,000[127]. Since the interactions are private, final sales figures aren't publicized, but the price of admission is high. It's not scaring young buyers away. In fact, they're the ones driving the trends.

"Contrary to what some of the alarm sounders may say, [young buyers] are not just buying modern stuff," he said. "If anything, the guys who are closer to middle age are way more guilty of buying stuff that's 10 years old or less. The younger guys are buying cars that are 30 years old or more. They're buying things that come from a time that they didn't even know. What does a guy in his early 30s know about that stuff? They weren't born until decades later."

Ivanhoe theorizes that social media has an outsized influence. Thousands of vintage car photos are posted to the app every day, exposing a younger generation to history that might have taken them years to discover on their own. There are so many people on Instagram that trends can spread like a California wildfire, shared by teens en masse until they reach the older users who actually do have the means to give Ivanhoe a meaningful car.

When something is hot online, it's really hot. The air-cooled Porsche movement remains in full swing. "If I put up a picture of a Ferrari 500 Superfast it might be a fantastic photo," Ivanhoe said, "but the engagement will be half of what I get from a Porsche 356 or an early air-cooled 911 of similar quality. That in itself becomes a feedback loop. They see that it gets attention and they say hey that looks cool."

It can be hard work for older generations to keep up with the patterns and whims of social media, but for Millennials and Gen Z, it's second nature. And catering to that crowd is giving Ivanhoe the upper hand as his business grows. Within the first year of launching, The Cultivated Collector Instagram account had 18,000 followers. By the two-year mark it had 26,000. Right after word of mouth, Instagram is his second-most important method for finding customers. Ivanhoe says he's found buyers for multi-million dollar cars off of Instagram posts. The account provides access to a pool of customers that competitors without social media presences simply don't have. The app is so fully populated that it can be hard to start from scratch now. "They're late to the party," he said.

Instagram purveyors like Ivanhoe and its hordes of car-crazy users are not only reacting to the market—they're influencing and driving the fluctuation of real-world prices. In addition to the usual suspects like classic Ferraris or supercars hitting the 20 to 30-year nostalgia mark, the cars that are experiencing the most fervent rise are of the thirst-trap ilk that always does great on Instagram: Fiats, Lancias, Alfa Romeos and air-cooled Porsches to the top of the list. The E30 M3 and its E36 successor. Anything that Group B breathed on is having a moment.

As long as enthusiasts have a place to come together and obsess over vehicles like those, whether it's Instagram or whatever mega-micro platform comes hot on its heels, there will be demand that hinges on the preferences of its users. It's allowing awe-worthy cars to be appreciated in their own time, before they become priceless historical artifacts decades from now.

"Things that were cool when new have a way of becoming legendary," Ivanhoe said.

Chapter XI: Patron Saint

For the longest time, no one knew what to make of the BMW E30 M3. Sure, it was a pretty little car, with two doors, a wide stance and big curvy hips. The E30 M3 exuded quickness. Its narrow, wedgy front end boasted quintessential '80s charisma. And besides, it was great to drive. Built from 1986 to 1991 as a high-powered version of the E30 3-Series sedan, the E30 M3 had a stiffer chassis, better suspension and more power from the four-cylinder engine.

They were great for racing on the cheap—and that's what people did with them. In the 1990s and 2000s it was common to find multiple E30 M3s screaming around corners—or brushing up against one another—at any track day in America. The car could take a beating and owners demanded it. They were for hardcore track rats. Why would you want an E30 M3 if you didn't intend to run the wheels off it? By the time car collectors were brushing themselves off after the Great Recession a decade ago, it was difficult to find an E30 M3 that hadn't been chopped, stripped, heavily modified or altogether beat to hell.

But then a funny thing happened—people began to covet the car. In 2010 a healthy E30 M3 would run you about $15,000 if you wanted a durable old sports car with good bones. Even if you wanted a virgin version that had been babied its entire life, it wouldn't cost you a second mortgage. In 2012, the best examples on the market drew about $25,000, tops.

Less than three years later, though, the market turned upside down. In 2014, a car with 69,000 miles sold for $58,000 on the online auction site BringATrailer.com. That same car that topped out at $25,000 in 2012 would cost you $67,900 in 2015, according to the Hagerty Price Guide.

It didn't stop there. The auction house Gooding & Company sold an '89 M3 convertible for $77,000[128] and then a '91 M3 convertible for $88,000[129].

Convertibles! No one even likes convertibles. You can't race them. They're heavier and less aerodynamic. So what are you going to do with them? The answer, it turns out, is store them in a garage and watch them appreciate.

Bonhams, another auction house, sold a coupe for $96,250[130]. By the time a low-mileage E30 M3 went for $102,000[131] on Bring A Trailer in 2018, nearly $40,000 more than the next-most expensive E30 M3 on the site, the trend couldn't be ignored.

"It's totally undriveable," said Warren Madsen, one of four regular hosts on the podcast *Driving While Awesome*, during a 2018 episode. "The person who bought that E30 has a frickin' warehouse."

The car had been a favorite of the group for its low cost, high performance and willingness to take a beating. Now, they're left to reconcile the idea of their beloved workhorse as the prized centerpiece in some tech founder's climate-controlled mausoleum. The hosts struggled to come to terms with the E30 M3 becoming the hottest commodity in collector cars. For the next 30 minutes, live on the show, the group went around and each named three cars they would buy instead for a total of $102,000. The episode is titled "BMW E30 M3 For $102K! We Can Do Better Than That."

Several things sparked the E30 M3 craze. First, people began to reflect on the E30 M3's legacy. The car won hundreds of races during its life span. It won across continents and driving styles, and it did so with old-school grit. In the '80s, automakers turned to turbocharging to punch up their small displacement engines, yet the E30 M3 remained naturally aspirated. While competitors sported advanced all-wheel drive systems that enabled their cars to launch out of corners, the E30 M3 only drove the rear wheels. Even as motorsports began to embrace the digital age during this time, the M3 was delightfully analog. It took drivers who were both clever and brave to push the lightweight Beamer to its limits. And when they did, the results were undeniable.

Second, the Internet and social media helped people rediscover the car. The E30 M3 was never a traditionally fast car—in its quickest edition, the car put down 0-60 mph runs in 6.5 seconds[132]. This was during a time when the Ferrari F40 and Porsche 959 sliced that in half. But the M3 delivered maximum driving enjoyment, was relatively attainable and could absolutely destroy its competition around the track. It has an estimated Nürburgring time of 8:08.70[133], more than six seconds better than the Audi Sport Quattro it was designed to beat. While Americans in the '80s remained stuck in the idea that stuffing the largest engine that could fit under the hood was the way to go, others recognized that light weight and a stiff chassis made a more complete package.

"As time has gone on, more and more enthusiasts, and especially this younger generation of enthusiasts, is really pulling away from this old notion of bigger is better, more is better, that quantity and size aren't necessarily everything," says Kim, the analyst who studies performance cars.

"The E30 M3 is absolutely an icon of that time period. It was a highly valuable car back then and it's once again back in the spotlight. People are not just remembering how awesome that car was but we have rediscovered how awesome it still is."

All of that means the car is tremendous to drive, and in recent years there is nothing more important than feel, responsiveness and driving enjoyment. The E30 M3 has all of those in spades. By the time the Bring A Trailer car crossed the $100k mark, the E30 M3 had been elevated to god-like status among Internet forums and particularly young people, buoying its legend and encouraging buyers who remembered the E30 M3 from their childhood but hadn't had the cash to get one.

If there is a patron saint of "Slow car fast," it is the BMW E30 M3.

*

It started with humble roots. In 1982, BMW launched the second generation of its famous 3-Series small sedan, codenamed "E30." The first generation, or the E21 3-Series, had cemented BMW as a global power and status symbol around the world. BMW took the E30 to new heights. Though they were low on muscle, making between 89 and 103 horsepower, the E30 3-Series had solid bones. The car was light and had responsive steering. Its suspension provided a soft ride for cruising and it had capabilities far beyond what most drivers would use in everyday situations. It was a great slow car. The one thing it needed was a fast version.

In the early '80s when the E30 3-Series debuted, a revolution was already underway. Audi had released its innovative Quattro all-wheel drive system on a stubby two-door nicknamed the Ur-Quattro. A technological marvel, Quattro allowed drivers to scramble out of any turn on any driving surface with great speed. It helped Audi earn serious bragging rights in European motorsports. The Quattro won dozens of rallies, touring car races and hill climbs using advanced technology to propel an otherwise common street car.

Meanwhile, a more direct competitor to BMW emerged with a shot across the bow. Mercedes pumped up its 190E entry sedan—the precursor to today's C-Class—with a powerful 2.3-liter engine with 16 valves. Hence its cumbersome name: the 190E 2.3-16. Engine specialists Cosworth built the motor, helping the car achieve 0-60 mph in, shockingly, under eight seconds. It made an impressive 185 horsepower[134]. Production began in 1984[135] following a series of production sedan high-speed records that led to whispers of the monster-beating sports saloon out of Stuttgart. Ahead of its launch, Mercedes-Benz provided 20 identical 190E 2.3-16s to Formula One drivers at the Nürburgring. A virtual unknown driver named Ayrton Senna smoked the field—adding to the car's rapidly growing legend. Racing fans were put on notice that the driver, and the car, were not to be taken lightly. The publicity stunts worked, but they also caught the eye of the competition. By the time the 190E 2.3-16 emerged ready for production in 1984, BMW was already deep into work on a project of its own.

BMW created the M3 solely so that it could enter the racing circuit. The only reason the M3 was even made available to the public as a road car is that the Fédération Internationale du Sport Automobile, or FISA, required automakers to sell 5,000 vehicles to the public in order to enter touring car championships. This is known as "homologation," a fancy way of saying,

"Convince the public to buy a bunch of street-legal racecars and we'll let you compete with it."

Racing was the whole point. As BMW prepared to sell the E30 M3 publicly, they also readied the M3 racecar. In November of 1986, as they prepared to enter the rally series known as Group A, executives named the newest batch of drivers in the Junior BMW Motorsport program. The M3 race drivers were given an exclusive look at the car and were asked to fine-tune its development. Among them was a 25-year old driver from Belgium named Eric van de Poele.

"It was a bit like Christmas time," Van de Poele told me. Van de Poele was still an amateur at the time, having not yet earned a full-time seat as a professional. The opportunity to not just drive, but to contribute to engineering the flagship racecar of BMW's future, was a dream come true.

"The M3 was a new step in the vision of the Group A category," Van de Poele told me. "BMW had developed this car with racing championships in mind, and so, even the road car was so much better than the competition. We proved directly that in fact, it was the car to beat."

Immediately upon its debut in 1986, the E30 M3 brought Mercedes a fight on the track. Across classes, styles and disciplines, the E30 M3 took victory in rallies, professional touring car series and amateur events all over the world. But the main goal was a Group A title.

Racing against turbocharged entries like the Ford Sierra and Volvo 240, as well as its arch-nemesis, the Mercedes 190E 2.3-16, the M3 stormed to the top in the touring car series. Its superb handling, acceleration out the corners and bulletproof toughness were difficult to beat right away. In the first race of the DTM season, a track-based series for German manufacturers, BMW took three of the top four spots.

"We knew that we were not the fastest in the straight compared to the turbo engines," Van de Poele said. "But the handling and of course the reliability could offer us a big plus."

The M3 won five out of 10 races in its first year[136]. When it was all said and done, even though he hadn't won a race all season, Van de Poele took the 1987 DTM driver's championship[137] in an M3. Adding up all the points it earned across multiple cars, BMW toppled Mercedes and easily captured the team title.

Success in DTM proved that the M3 formula was a winner, but that was far from the only supporting evidence. In 1987 alone, the E30 M3 also won season championships in Australia, at the European Touring Car Championship and at the World Touring Car Championship. It won rallies in France[138] and on the Isle of Man[139]. Videos of Belgian rally driver Peter Snijers tossing the M3 sideways around impossible turns in 1988 became the stuff of legend and only fed the fire of E30 M3 cult fandom[140]. In those videos, Snijers looks more like he's hanging onto a fire-breathing dragon for dear life than driving your dentist's 3-Series.

It won DTM again in 1989. It emerged victorious at the 24 Hours of Nürburgring (four times[141]) and the 24 Hours of Spa, in Belgium (also four times)[142]. BMW claims the car has won more than 1,500 races in total. If you want to make a case that the BMW E30 M3 is the greatest road racing car of all time—and many do—it is difficult to argue.

"Driving for a factory like BMW was unbelievable," says Van de Poele. After his DTM title in the M3 put him on the map, he went from semi-pro to high demand. He won Spa five times, Le Mans three times and the 12 Hours of Sebring twice[143]. He also had short stints in Formula One. "I learned everything at BMW and they have been the key to my career."

Its success on the track immediately translated to sales in the showroom. The plan, according to James Taylor's book *BMW M3, The Complete Story*, was to build the first 5,000 for homologation as quickly as possible and then taper off production to meet demand. But the first production run ended just as the M3 started winning in DTM. It became a hot commodity—as a super-fast "saloon," or family sedan, but also as a status symbol for the wealthy. BMW upped its numbers. They green-lighted a lighter and faster version called the M3 Evolution, so they could race it, of course, and built the entire run of 500 in three months. In 1988 the company decided to add a convertible version, launched the M3 Evolution II and began selling the M3 in the U.S. and Japan.

By the time production of the E30 M3 ended for good in 1991, BMW had sold a total of 17,970 around the world—more than triple the original estimate. There were six special editions that combined to sell an extra 2,259 units. The M3 marked an incredible run of unexpected success for BMW, stuffing its pockets with enormous profit margins and bolstering its brand pedigree as the most performance you could get for the money. That reputation is still what is selling the car today.

"The racing pedigree is certainly a big draw," says Eric Keller, owner of Enthusiast Auto Group, a restoration shop and seller in Cincinnati. Since founding EAG in 2000, Keller has turned the company into the most distinguished restorer of pristine M3 cars outside of the automaker's own BMW Classic division. Keller specializes in the E30 M3, taking the vintage machines and lovingly returning them to nearly factory fresh quality with excruciating attention to detail. All this comes at a price. EAG is not the place for people upset at the idea of a $100,000 M3.

In 18 years, Keller estimates he has completed more than 300 sales of E30 M3s on the private market. And a Keller product does not come cheap. Cars of the ultra-high class quality that were selling for $60,000-70,000 in 2013 are now easily clearing $180,000, he said. At the time of our conversation, the EAG website offered an original, single-owner 1988 E30 M3, white body on red interior, with 8,000 miles. List price: $199,999. It sold in weeks. Special editions go for even more, at undisclosed prices. Keller simultaneously listed six Evolution models, all requesting calls to inquire about price, including a 1989 Johnny Cecetto Edition[144] of which only 480 were made.

"We're selling way better cars than what the auctions have access to," Keller says. According to his estimates, it takes about $15,000 and 200-300 hours of work to bring an E30 M3 up to his standards.

"A good percentage of EAG buyers have owned an E30 M3 before. If they didn't have one back then, they wanted one. The car is good enough that someone wants to own it multiple times, spending four to five-times more than when they sold it. That's hard for a lot of guys, but they're willing to do it. The majority of people buying them over the last 5-6 years are in the 30 to 55 age range. Now that the demographic is coming into their money they're buying what they've always wanted, and the E30 M3 is the whole story. The E30 M3 is just one of the most enjoyable sports cars ever made. It's hard for that car to not leave a smile on your face once you drive it. You feel like you're a racecar driver."

It's difficult to say whether the E30 M3 market has peaked. Keller calls it "pretty darn strong." The car could well end up being a true all-time collectible, fetching quarter-million dollar prices 30 years from now as the few remaining low mileage cars are scooped up and locked away. But it will truly be interesting to see whether the effect is recreated on its successors. The E30 M3 didn't merely stand alone for very long; it launched successors that made the M3 the most heralded line of cars in BMW history.

In 1992 the E36 M3 offered more comfort and luxury but added a six-cylinder engine. Perhaps its turn is coming on the nostalgia circuit, but for now the E36 is following the track-beater stereotype that the E30 M3 originally set forth. Very good examples can be had for under $20,000 and top cars from EAG are still under $30k. In 2000, the E46 M3 came with a similar straight-six juiced to an incredible 338 horsepower. Its handling was so far and away ahead of its time that *Road & Track* named the car its favorite sports car of all-time. Considering this pedigree, its attractive styling and the fact that it was the final naturally-aspired six-cylinder M3, the E46 M3 could be headed for an explosion that rivals the E30 version. Most currently sell for about $20,000-30,000 on Bring A Trailer[145]. Only one has cracked $50k.

Perhaps the biggest thing holding prices of the E46 M3 back is that BMW sold 85,000 of them worldwide, about four times more than sales of the E30 M3. BMW sold more E46 M3s—a high-performance sports car for the wealthy—than Chrysler sold of its budget-friendly 200 sedan over the final three years of its production[146]. With that kind of supply, it's difficult to envision a future where the E46 M3 is regularly fetching triple-digit prices. But you never know.

It also puts into perspective how rare and unique the E30 M3 was. As the true originator of the trend, a charter member of "Slow car fast" and at less than 18,000 sold (out of 2.3 million E30s total[147]), there is a strong argument to be made that even current going rates for the E30 M3 are drastically undervalued. Not only should the E30 M3 be worth more money, it is exactly the kind of car that is deserving of such demand. Car enthusiasts have spent years arguing that the true value of a car is when you strip away the hype, the celebrity factor, the badge on the front and the magazine covers, what makes a car truly valuable is the experience it delivers to the driver. While current prices may be tough to swallow, the acceleration of E30 M3 costs should be viewed as validation to its fans that they're right. They won. The legend of the E30 M3 is being recognized and rewarded. There are more than 160,000 posts on Instagram with the #E30M3 hashtag—there are 18,000 with #UrQuattro and, understandably, 3,000 with #190E16v. Enthusiasts and collectors are smarter now. They aren't throwing wads of cash indiscriminately at cars that have a fancy name. Hype machines like the Ferrari Testarossa[148] have stalled while one-niche cult classics like the Toyota 2000GT and Mazda RX-7 have sky-rocketed. Isn't the E30 M3 the posterchild for an informed car culture?

"It has the racing pedigree and is perhaps the very best example of this idea of 'slow car fast,'" Kim says. "One-hundred and ninety horsepower—quick, but nothing Earth-shattering on paper. The magic was in driving it; it was so much more than the sum of its parts. It's an icon of that era because despite not being a particularly super-fast car it was certainly one of the most fun and enjoyable cars of that era. For driver involvement and feeling in the experience at that time period, what could touch it? Its iconic status is absolutely deserved."

*

The BMW E30 M3's creators were not so torn about the car. They simply wanted something that would elevate the common 3-Series, push the boundaries of grip and absolutely dominate on the track. And they had the perfect person to guide the effort.

Thomas Ammerschlager seemed destined to build sports cars. He chose the career path at age seven, he told the German-language magazine *Capri Club Deutschland* in 2017, and never looked back.

Ammerschlager earned a mechanical engineering degree and by 1970 jumped straight into racing, taking a position as the chassis engineer in the test department at NSU Motorenwerke AG, then a small manufacturer of cars and motorcycles. Ammerschlager was responsible for developing the company's Prinz racecar. He was also the driver and won several times, including a 15-lap race at the famed Hockheimring by an impressive 10 seconds[149]. Pictures from the era show the portly man stuffed into a tiny tin Prinz 1100 TT hustling the car around the tarmac. You can nearly hear the tires screaming through the photos.

Ford hired Ammerschlager away to assist with the next version of its successful racecar, the Capri RS. For the 1973 season Ford wanted to make the car stiffer, but the rules forbade changing the car's length, width or any of its dimensions. So how? By venturing outside the rules, Ammerschlager told *Capri Club.*

Here, Ammerschlager demonstrated his unique style of thinking.

He and the team welded a racing cage into the car—which was prohibited—and stuck fake screw heads to the cage at the normal connection points to fool inspectors into thinking they held it in place[150], Ammerschlager wrote in *Automobilsport.* The welded cage reinforced the extra stability he had already built into the car, and helped the suspension do its job better as well.

The car was renowned for its safety. Formula One champion Jackie Stewart, a notorious advocate for safety in his day, called the Capri "the first car I feel really safe in." But in 1978 another challenge arose. The Capri racing program had been taken up by the racing team Zakspeed and was promptly embarrassed by turbocharged BMWs. Zakspeed needed to find a solution. Ammerschlager looked for new ways to increase grip, so drivers could hold higher speeds through the corners. He built a 1:5 model of the car and rented space at a nearby wind tunnel. The car began to take on new shapes: huge fenders, a big rear wing and low front spoilers. The new body produced huge amounts of downforce, coupled with a unique rear wing shape that pushed the car to the ground even through drifting. The car promptly won eight out of ten races, however at the end of the season the series deemed the rear wing too effective and stripped driver Klaus Ludwig of the title.

Fine, Ammerschlager thought. For 1981 he ditched the big wing and focused instead on the underside of the car. He took airflow tunnels under the car and cranked them up higher[151]. Porsche had an extra 200 horsepower over the Capri that season. It didn't matter. Porsche couldn't copy the design because of its rear engine and BMW couldn't replicate it due to a low rear axle. Zakspeed won 10 out of 13 races and the championship in 1981.

Ammerschlager left the Capri program in 1982 for Audi. An early project was crafting the Ur-Quattro, one of the most revolutionary performance cars of its era, an unstoppable force in rallying and a future rival of the E30 M3. After his undeniable success at Audi he was scooped up by BMW as technical director of the M group. The knowledge gained from tuning touring cars, skirting racing regulations and perfecting aerodynamics throughout his career were about to come in very handy.

Development began in 1983. Ammerschlager and the M team started with the E30 3-Series and began to nip and tuck. They added wider fenders and tires. They added a rear wing and low front spoiler for downforce. They saved weight by thinning the glass in the rear and side windows. The car weighed just 2,833 pounds—a fraction of the heft of today's hypercars.

Under the hood, Ammerschlager simply took what they had and made it better. The four-cylinder had two overhead camshafts, four valves and a centrally located spark plug. Instead of reinventing the wheel with more valves per cylinder, Ammerschlager opted to increase the bore of the engine, which increases power at the high end and makes for a rev-happy engine. It was the equivalent of tapping a nail with a sledgehammer.

Ammerschlager changed every body panel from the E30 3-Series except for the roof and hood[152]. The car's coefficient of drag fell from 0.36 to 0.33, making it more slick through the air. Its shape and contoured lines were so dramatic that BMW's reserved executives were nearly frightened into watering it down. The suspension was completely different; the steering was more direct[153]. Ammerschlager altered the interior of the car to simplify the process of adding a roll cage—one installed in adherence with the rules this time.

"I would be very happy to see him and let him know that I never told him enough how good his M3 was," van de Poele says. "And how much it helped my career."

As for the sudden popularity of the E30 M3, van de Poele is not surprised. Perhaps it just needed time to bloom. When it comes to vehicles that truly changed our collective idea of how a performance car should act, the Audi Ur-Quattro was more revolutionary. The Mercedes 190E 2.3-16, with its landmark 16-valve design, came two years earlier. But the E30 M3 remains the gold standard.

"If I could, I'd be most happy to drive one every day," van de Poele says. "The funny side is that it once was the routine. Today, a dream."

Chapter XII: Form or Die

There is no more subjective aspect to a car than its looks. Is it cool? Is it ugly? Is it futuristic? Is it copying a trend? Are those intakes too big? Are the lines distracting? Ask 100 people and you will get 100 answers.

Making a car pretty or interesting or cool, can seem like an easy job. But to the people who do it, the task can be all-consuming. Before a vehicle makes it to the showroom, car designers have poured years of their lives into every detail. Every curve, every scoop, every headlamp case and handle shape and bumper style has been sketched thousands of times. Then, it's been scrutinized by sharp-tongued supervisors and executives and sent back for revision.

Marketing: "We can't sell that, make it do this." Engineering: "We can't build that, make it do that." Accounting: "We can't afford that, make it do this." Being a car designer means being a people-pleaser.

And sometimes, first impressions of a new design don't do it justice. When I first saw pictures of the McLaren 720S online, I thought it looked ungainly. To my eye, the cabin seemed stretched too far forward. The headlight-in-intake design looked gimmicky. The whole thing seemed to scream "I'm a supercar!" Supercars shouldn't need to convince me, I thought. They should make me believe.

In photos, the 720S seemed desperate to be noticed. But in person my opinion changed. The exaggerated proportions cast eye-popping shadows across every surface. The intake airflow follows an intricate weave pattern through scoops and inlets that resonate in power and agility. It oozes style. The thing just makes sense.

"It's about removing excess," said Alex Alexiev, a senior designer at McLaren. Born in Bulgaria, his family immigrated to the U.S. in 1996. As a teenager Alexiev hung posters of the vaunted McLaren F1 on the walls of his bedroom in Fort Meyers, Florida. Now 29, he's part of the team that designed the 720S as well as the brand's 650, 675LT, vehicles in the high-performance MSO line of supercars and the almighty Senna. Alexiev has been at McLaren for five years, working out of the company's iconic spaceship-inspired headquarters in Woking, 30 miles outside London.

Alexiev's situation is unique in several ways. It normally takes years for even the most visionary designers to work their way up to designing a single performance car—let alone an entire lineup of supercars for a dedicated exotic and racecar manufacturer. Additionally, when a designer is hired at a major manufacturer they can expect to be one of hundreds. At a large operation like Ford, Toyota or General Motors there are some 250-300 designers stationed around the world.

When Alexiev was hired at McLaren he became one of five. Since then, the design team has expanded to nine. "I never expected McLaren to be an option," Alexiev told me. "It was always just a dream with no chance of being possible. I figured I'd join GM or Toyota. When the McLaren thing came up I thought, 'What the hell is going on?'"

Alexiev's path to McLaren is out of the ordinary, but it was no accident. Well-connected in the auto industry, he met McLaren's then-head of design Frank Stephenson when he talked his way into the launch of the P1 hybrid hypercar in Beverly Hills. Alexiev introduced himself and slipped the executive his portfolio. A week later he had an interview and became part of the tiny team tasked with reshaping the look and feel of an automotive titan.

"There's no time to work on concept stuff," Alexiev said. "There's satisfaction in knowing that what you're doing will be product. That being said, you're looking after things like a full interior by yourself. It's a lot of work but it's really worth it as a designer because of the ownership and control of the delivery. You literally follow it through from initial kickoff to rolling off the production line. We don't have a three-to-five year design cycle—everything at McLaren is considerably faster, in some cases 18 months from start to finish to do a whole car. That's where time management comes in. All those things I learned at ArtCenter."

The ArtCenter, or ArtCenter College of Design, is perhaps the most esteemed of a select handful of places to learn automotive design in the world. Nestled high up in the hills of Pasadena, California, its modernist steel architecture shaded by towering maple trees, ArtCenter has produced scores of influential car designers. The alumni list ranges from customizer Chip Foose to Ferrari Enzo designer Ken Okuyama and polarizing BMW legend Chris Bangle. The lineage stretches back to Pete Brock who practically defined American racing in the 1960s with his Corvette Sting Ray and Shelby Daytona Cobra Coupe.

Graduating from ArtCenter carries a lot of cache. So it was much more than a chance meeting with Frank Stephenson that earned Alexiev a foot in the door at McLaren. An undergraduate degree from ArtCenter is an endorsement that this person can handle stinging critique, work in aggressive environments and bring professional workplace experience to the table. The coursework is demanding and access is limited. Across 11 undergraduate and seven graduate programs, the current ArtCenter enrollment is only 2,100 total students[154]. It's also expensive. Current tuition is more than $20,000 per term, or $40,000 per year[155], not including the demanding cost of tools and supplies. As a student, Alexiev had to take off every third term to work as a valet at the local Ritz-Carlton to keep up with expenses.

Even to Alexiev, who was described to me by his former professors as "special" and "clearly destined to design cars," the rigorous demands of school took a toll. "In five years at McLaren I've done three or four all-nighters," he said. "At ArtCenter, three or four a week. For five years."

I paid a visit to ArtCenter during the 2018 summer term to see first-hand how the private, nonprofit college prepares the next generation of car designers. As you turn onto campus and follow a winding two-lane road the main building comes into view, its most prominent feature a towering bridge of diagonal steel beams looming over the road. The idea behind the architecture was to create an environment for fostering creativity with a foundation of hard, serious work.

"The focus was on course work, not extracurricular activities, with few places for meetings and community gatherings," reads the college's official history of its 1974 campus construction[156]. The building never sleeps. It's common to find students in classrooms or using machining facilities deep into the night, or catching fleeting naps under their work stations.

I parked at the north end of campus and crossed the open-air bridge, past the main lobby and rotating museum of student work, to reach the south wing. Just before noon I reached the unadorned door to the classroom at Room 216. Inside, I walked into a hurricane of designs. Hand-drawn sketches, colorful renderings and glossy computer-generated images coated every corkboard wall in a space the size of a small warehouse. The students who had posted them milled about. They started showing up hours ago, preparing their latest work for review and critique, meticulously spacing the drawings on the wall for the best possible visibility.

It was Week 6 in the semester, which meant each student had by now selected a project, defined its mission and were well into the design process. Today was about refining the overall shape and style and introducing a "lighting signature," or how the headlights and taillights will look to fit the rest of the car. There were coupes, sedans, urban mobility vehicles, one-seat exotics and flying cars set in 2050. These were Term 8 students, meaning the seniors ready to graduate. Commencement was just weeks away. They wore plain tees and jeans, or billowy denim shirts and loose khakis artfully rolled up past the ankle. Nearly all wore Adidas sneakers. They had been through the ringer and were about to emerge on the other side with a degree worth its weight in lucrative job offers. To me, each design looked incredible. Ready for production. Ship it.

But there was no time for students to admire their own work. Being so close to the finish line meant it was crucial to keep the projects moving forward. Any revisions that need to be made will steal valuable time away from completion. In a few weeks, the students were expected to present finished renderings and physical models at the annual college showcase for the public. This review of lighting signatures could fast-track their project for completion or shove it into a thicket of back-tracking and those infamous all-nighters. I pulled up a stool and waited for the instructor.

*

Jason Hill is an ArtCenter alumni and has been a faculty member for more than a decade. Early in his professional career, Hill became famous for the design of the Porsche Carrera GT concept that debuted at the 2000 Paris Auto Show. By the end of that week Porsche had more than 100 orders in hand from customers before it even announced its cost. Hill also led the team that eventually brought the production version to life in 2005. Soon after, he left Porsche and worked a few gigs before starting his own firm, Design By 11, in 2010, allowing him the freedom to choose his own projects as well as teach.

As he walked into Room 216, Hill, a slight and well-crafted 51-year-old with glasses and a friendly but incisive demeanor, held the next few weeks of his students' sleep in his hands. Hill has seen it all. You want to impress him but get the feeling he knows what you're going to say before you say it. On this Friday afternoon—ArtCenter students have long lost hope of any weekend social life—Hills sends his students a warm welcome and invites them to present their work.

The process goes like this: each student takes turns standing in front of Hill and the rest of the class, delivering a re-hash of their project and then showing the latest progress, pointing to pertinent sketches hung on the wall to trace the evolution. You sell your progress, essentially. There are lots of approaches to presenting, and a lot of ways to explain yourself out of or into trouble. But the drawings don't lie. Presenting design work is laying out the last few weeks of your life to be torn to pieces in front of your peers. These students know the deal. They are among the finest designers and most skilled artists at the most prestigious creative school in the country, possibly the world. They've been working relentlessly to hone their project for Hill's approval. And they've walked into a bloodbath.

One by one, Hill makes his way around the room.

"Your part lines are way out of scale."

"I don't know if your face is there yet and you're trying to force this grille."

"You can't have blue lights. You're not a cop."

"Render in that wheel intrusion so it doesn't feel like a train."

"Is that green or grey?" "It's grey," the student responds. "It's a really bad grey."

"I'm going to give you very clear instructions. Not suggestions. Instructions. Do these again. And then throw them away and do them again."

No project is safe. Each student receives their share of criticism and will have to go back to the drawing board. In the middle of one critique, Hill stands up and asks for designer tape, a thin and flexible type of tape that can be easily shaped to map out proportions on a two-dimensional drawing. He takes to the side profile sketches of one student's project and, using the tape, begins to alter its most prominent lines and shapes to demonstrate the direction that should be taken moving forward. Soon, other students are joining in, suggesting lines and pulling tape across drawings as their classmate, in the middle of his presentation, can only watch his week's worth of work be dissected and redrawn in front of him.

The stress can be gut-wrenching, but taken as a whole, the process is a net-positive for young designers who are trying to work out kinks before they reach the big stage. Here, they can make mistakes and earn valuable feedback about where they're going wrong. There won't be as much room for error in the drafting room at Honda. Every student that has made it to Term 8 has been through years of critiques just like this one. And every student in Room 216 has completed at least one professional internship. They already know how the inside of an automotive design studio works. They know what they need to do to get better.

*

The discussions that arise from the critiques provide an insightful look into the ways that car design will continue to evolve and adapt to a changing automotive landscape. Hill, like all instructors in the Transportation Design department, can be scathing and demanding. But he makes it clear there is a purpose behind each note. There are several consistent themes that continually drive his remarks. One is the need to communicate a clear brand identity, such as when he instructs students to make their Cadillac badge larger or make their front styling less like Toyota's current models. Another is to build on established foundational elements of design, like traditional coupe proportions or wheelhouse styles in place since the 1960s.

One of the most important themes he presses is exploring new thoughts and ideas, even if they don't seem feasible. One after another, Hill encourages his students to experiment with translucent surfaces, integrating roll cages into the vehicle structure and building a Swiffer-style sliding roof liner into a family-friendly crossover concept. Everything is grounded in reality—or at least our perception of what reality will look like one day—but the point is to push boundaries. It's easy to listen to Hill preach progressiveness and believe that while we'll always have the Camry, the Camry of tomorrow might be unrecognizable from the Camry of today.

Out of necessity, designers traffic in the future. Their designs have to be at least five years from hitting the road, and often closer to 10 to 15 years. Between critiques, the class routinely discusses the role of cars moving forward. One of the ideas frequently kicked around Room 216 is that vehicles will increasingly be pushed away from a do-it-all style and toward specialized use cases.

"With autonomous vehicles, there might only be two places in the future where you can pilot your own vehicle—one is on a track and the other is off-road," Hill told me. "It will designed for these specific things."

In the future, will we be outlawed from manually driving our cars on public roads? Will we be required to turn our Jeep Wrangler Rubicons into Autonomous mode until we reach the desert? Will our Porsche GT3RS automatically drive itself until it reaches the confines of a racetrack? Right now it's too early to tell, but the idea is being openly discussed inside design schools. They have to be prepared for it.

"Each car is going to be very focused on what they're built for," one student told me. "A sports car is going to feel very specialized for performance. That's my guess if I had to bet."

An autonomous future and the proliferation of performance are both having an impact on the way our cars look. Increasingly, however, vehicle style will be dictated by electrification, and the theme proliferated across the student designs. Felipe Garcia designed a battery-powered Honda SUV that, without the need for a traditional engine, utilized more space for passengers and storage with shorter front and rear bumpers. Ivan Palacios Rey presented an electric 2035 Jeep that stores motors in the floor to keep a low center of gravity while still boasting tall ground clearance.

The role of electrification has already reached real-world design. When McLaren built the 903-horsepower electric-hybrid P1 in 2013 it included enlarged scoops to feed an upgraded radiator and tons of mesh-covered openings to ensure proper cooling. Many of these design features have filtered into other, non-hybrid McLaren models. As the brand moves toward its goal of 100 percent hybridization by 2035, they will only become more common.

And as the use of electric battery power continues, cooling will be a predominant aspect of vehicle design, Alexiev told me. "Heat soaks around the engine bay and inlets," he said. As a result, the control of airflow is crucial. You can add scoops and wings to increase drag and grip. Or you can smooth the surface to chase top speed. "The aero story of the car changes depending on whether the car is going on the track, versus a low-drag situation for acceleration and top speed."

Either way, it's critical that the vehicle's power source—whether battery-electric or traditional engines—remains cool. Batteries and electric motors add weight. So do electronic parts, infotainment systems and federally-regulated safety equipment. The heavier a vehicle gets the more power it takes to motivate, and the more heat it generates. If you add all that weight without managing cooling it's not going to last long. For all the incredible performance Tesla has engineered into its fully-electric cars, at full bore on a racetrack they only last a select number of laps before flashing warnings to cool down.

Student work proves performance look is coming to all cars whether it has an actual effect on performance or not. But there's another trend occurring inside exotic design studios that could have a very real effect on the way we look at cars. The growth of technologies like virtual reality and three-dimensional printing are at the root of a revolution for car designers. With virtual reality they are able to build and view a reasonable facsimile of their design in a real-world environment in minutes, moving it around to view angles and proportions and make adjustments on the fly. Meanwhile, 3D printing allows students and designers to quickly manufacture parts and components that can be fitted to working models and tested before approving for production.

"In a day or two I can knock out three-to-four different themes to get an idea of proportion and packaging," Alexiev said. "We're using a lot of those virtual-reality sketch tools to quickly work through themes and get into position to work through volumes and surfaces."

The point is not to skip or replace sketching by hand. VR is not meant to eliminate rendering or even model-building. The point is to get through those steps faster. McLaren began using virtual reality to improve its design process in 2016. But there were still barriers to taking physical drawings and computer-generated images, and transferring them to VR. So McLaren built its own program. Called Vector Suite[157], it allows McLaren designers to build a three-dimensional vehicle with mechanical components and design the exterior around it. The vehicle can then bend and twist around its own parts, giving it realistic cause and effect. Vector Suite can transition between two-dimensional and three-dimensional designs, then seamlessly move to the 3D printing process. Doing things this way solves a lot of problems that normally are not sorted out until the concept is built into a time-consuming, life-sized clay model, Alexiev said.

"Clay will never go away," he said. "In our case, no one's going to sign off on a car without seeing it in the physical, painted up and made up to look real. You can't judge any of that in the virtual world, things are always different than they look on the screen. Sometimes you machine it out and say, 'Holy crap, we have to change every single surface.' It's the efficiency we're trying to improve on, not necessarily the process."

The tech provides McLaren with unheard of speed and flexibility. In some cases the company can go from approved concept to full production in 18 months. In 2017 Alexiev needed only five weeks to design the virtual McLaren Vision GT for the latest edition of the *Gran Turismo* video game series. The ability to adapt to design trends, or develop new ones on the fly, is a huge competitive advantage in an industry that typically takes years to fully realize design language.

McLaren is an anomaly. Its small design team allows quick turnarounds, and designers are typically involved in meetings and decisions throughout the development process alongside engineering, marketing and executives. This is practically unheard of at the large-scale automakers, where different departments sometimes don't even share space on the same campus. But even Ford and GM are reportedly all-in on virtual reality, too[158]. If the technology spreads across the industry the future of car design could be far more rapid and resistant to copying than in the past.

*

Back at ArtCenter, instructors like Hill are preparing students to use technology quickly, but on traditional timelines. In most cases the job of a designer has become akin to being a project manager.

"You're expected to wear many hats," one student told me. "I feel like the job is getting more spread out." It's not enough these days for designers to expect to focus solely on drawing.

"Design is something where everyone's an expert," Hill said. "They say, 'You should make it look like this.' You cannot leave the design studio and go suggest something to the finance department, but they will still come in and say 'Oh that looks great,' or 'That's ugly.' So it's an interesting thing you have to manage. As designers, whether we like it or not, everybody's invested in the look and the feel."

Automotive design is a demanding career with little fanfare. The work is rigorous and the pay is relatively low. For these students, the skill is a labor of love and the promise of a job is a dream. When I asked how many got into car design because of an existing love of cars, 13 out of the 14 students raised their hand. Hill will help them get there. Though his critiques are sharp, they are often buffered with praise and encouragement.

"The design process is about discovery and you've discovered the wrong direction. It's good. Now you can move to the right direction."

"Your lighting signatures are cool but I want your next design to do something really exciting. You did a good job with the proportion and package—that's where we live."

"Get rid of that part. It's cliché. Or it's not even cliché, it's just overdone. You're close though. Really close."

"I'm so glad you did your bad versions first. Now you're onto the good ones. And your next ones will be better."

"This feels lazy. Maybe a little more sophistication, more snap in the lines. That'd be cool!"

There are gems of wisdom in every note Hill delivers. True, you have to go through a lot of sweat and sleep deprivation to get the genuine praise. But designers will tell you that makes it worth it. Hill constantly congratulates his students for their abstract successes, in achieving an "essence" or a "smoothness" or an "enthusiasm" in their designs. He tells one student their surfaces are beautiful. He tells another not to post their work on Instagram until at least six months after they've been hired—their designs are too cutting-edge and will be stolen. There is clearly a lot of talent in the room and Hill takes care to provide valuable feedback they can use not only for this term but carry with them in their careers. There's an art to it.

And it's one the students are still learning. During one critique, Hill asks the class to provide their own thoughts on one person's work.

"What do we think?" he asks, awaiting an insightful response.

Silence. Some students look at their shoes, some blankly stare straight ahead. Hill doesn't flinch. He waits.

After several beats, a voice from the back.

"It's good."

Hill turns his chair to face the student who said it.

"It's... *good?*"

Chapter XIII: The Hard Part

In a 2016 race on the infield road course at the Indianapolis Motor Speedway, IndyCar driver Oriol Servia blasted down the back straight at speeds approaching 180 mph. Servia, originally from Spain, was 41 at the time and a veteran of IndyCar and other racing series. At this point in his career, Servia was looking for a consistent job. The race at Indy was his debut for the Schmidt Petersen Motorsports team, and he was determined to make a good impression.

Servia's Honda engine screamed all eight of its cylinders around a turn and unfurled to its top speed. Up ahead, out of the corner of his eye, he spotted one of the cars lose grip and make contact with the outside wall. It wasn't a bad wreck—a couple of carbon fiber bits made a big show of flying up into the air—and Servia would clear it without trouble. He zoomed by and continued on.

Approaching the next corner, Servia saw his teammate James Hinchcliffe approaching to make a pass. Hinchcliffe, a rising star on the circuit, was the face of Schmidt Petersen. He'd already worked his way through most of the pack and now needed to pass Servia to make a run at the top drivers. The two drivers barreled down the track when Servia noticed that Hinchcliffe was pushing him toward the grass. Racing drivers are used to being pressured by one another; they constantly jostle for position and work to gain advantages by the millimeter. Sometimes, that means you're about to get squeezed off the pavement.

But Hinchcliffe didn't have a reputation for driving like this. Plus, these two were teammates. Servia didn't know what to make of it. He gave Hinchcliffe as much room as he could, tightrope-walking along the edge of the track to allow him the space to make the pass. At perilous speed, Hinchcliffe's screaming car crept closer and closer until Servia couldn't give any more. "He keeps squeezing me, squeezing me, squeezing me," Servia recalled. The two cars touched tires.

Immediately, Hinchcliffe seemed to snap out of it. He relented space to Servia and both drivers slammed on the brakes to slow for the next corner. They continued on with proper space between themselves until it was safe to make a clear pass. Servia was confused. This was the Hinchcliffe he knew—not the super-aggro driver that had tried to push him out of the race a few corners ago.

What the hell happened?

Servia would learn the reason after the race. Before the incident, as the two drivers came around the corner and prepared to blast down the long straightaway, both had seen the car ahead that made contact with the wall. Servia sped out of harm's way but Hinchcliffe passed it a half-second later. Out of the dust and debris that spewed into the air, one of the pieces was the end plate, an aerodynamic flap about two feet long, one attached to the front wing and another to the rear wing that helps direct airflow and produce downforce. As the end plate tumbled through the air, gravity brought it down toward the track—right on top of Hinchcliffe in his open-air car. He never even saw it.

The end plate knocked Hinchcliffe unconscious right away. Dazed and with his foot pressed hard onto the throttle he unknowingly barreled down the straightaway and began drifting into Servia's space. "It was only when we touched wheels that woke him up," Servia said.

Servia told the story of his close encounter during a driver safety seminar held at the 2018 Toyota Grand Prix of Long Beach. More than 100 people crammed into a small conference room in the Long Beach Convention Center to attend. Many were young budding drivers who came with their parents to hear pro racers, safety engineers and medical experts discuss the risks of racing and preventative measures. IndyCar, IMSA and Pirelli World Challenge drivers tore down Pine Avenue just outside.

The seminar was hosted by the Stand 21 Foundation, a nonprofit arm of the Stand 21 racing apparel brand. Among the hottest topics at the conference was IndyCar's recent decision to adopt a new windshield, or "canopy," for its racecars in future seasons. Throughout its century-plus history, Indycar racing has been defined by its open-air top that exposes drivers to the elements. In the early days, about 1902 to 1925, drivers wore little protection on their head and face: a slim leather helmet, strapped snug under the chin, and a pair of goggles that covered their eyes but left the face caked in dirt, soot and bugs by the end of the drive. Six drivers were killed in the 1916 season alone.

Today, Indy drivers wear state-of-the-art lightweight helmets that are more aerodynamic and protective than ever. While far safer than a half-inch of leather, the helmets can't save drivers from everything they face on the track. A canopy certainly could have prevented the incident that knocked Hinchcliffe out at triple-digit speeds. Purists may decry the look and feel of the protective windshield, but one of the prevailing messages of the seminar was we know better. And we're learning more all the time.

"We need the canopy," Servia said. "It's probably 20 years too late but I'm happy it's happening. We need to constantly keep pushing. That's why I'm happy today—at least we talk about safety and people bring ideas and find new ways to make us safer. It's so important."

Indycar isn't alone in trying to better itself and the safety of its drivers. In 2016, IMSA eliminated all but one of its open-cockpit classes in favor of more advanced prototype racecars with fixed roofs. In 2018, Formula One began racing with a hoop-like structure called the "halo" that encircles the driver's helmet without affecting their vision. The storied 24 Hours of Le Mans introduced safety measures such as limits on the number of laps a driver can complete without a pit stop and a set amount of time before which they need to switch—moves spurred on by the extreme speeds and G-forces the top prototypes now exert on the human body.

Racing has always been fertile ground for innovation, with the results finding their way into passenger cars. Technologies like anti-lock brakes, turbochargers and superchargers and even rearview mirrors all came from the track first.

Lately, though, it's been the other way around: passenger cars are returning the safety technology favor. As horsepower has grown at a phenomenal rate the laws and techniques employed to keep greater speeds from harming people have become extremely advanced by necessity. The types of tests they conduct, the way they measure and collect data and especially the methods used to construct vehicles that are increasingly capable of break-neck speeds have all contributed to production cars that are safer than ever.

They have to be. In 2016, the Insurance Institute for Highway Safety, or IIHS, issued three alarming reports in quick succession: drivers with cars that have more horsepower are statistically more likely to speed[159]; rising speed limits lead to thousands of additional fatal accidents on U.S. roads every year[160]; and muscle cars—also statistically more likely to speed and more likely to crash—are less likely to perform well in crash tests[161].

As we struggle to deal with higher speeds and more power in everyday cars, safety measures and advancements are being asked to make up much of the difference. And in an odd twist, the lessons learned from building a safer Mustang are trickling across to the motorsports world, so that a 200-mph crash on the Mulsanne Straight is no longer a death sentence.

*

Servia wasn't even there to talk about the Hinchcliffe incident. He had come to explain the feeling of crashing in the Indy 500 in 2017, and watching his dream of winning the race slip away. Servia had been running in seventh place with 17 laps to go when he spun on the inside of Turn 1, collecting the car of James Davidson and sending them both into the wall. Two more cars crashed before the dust settled. Everyone emerged unscathed. "I had many, many crashes more scary than that one," Servia said. "This one I was just pissed because I really thought I had a shot at winning."

Jonnie Lindberg, a driver in the National Hot Rod Association (NHRA), dissected his drag race crash at the Arizona Nationals where opponent John Force's car exploded at 290 mph, slammed its enormous rear tire through Lindberg's windshield and pushed him head-first into the wall in a fiery mess of tangled parachutes[162]. After he was removed from the wreckage, Lindberg noticed a tire mark on his helmet. He'd been saved by the high-strength roll structure in his car. The next day he had only a sore neck.

"I guess I'm lucky," Lindberg said. "If the wheel comes into the cockpit, I'm not sitting here right now."

Courtney Crone, a teenage dirt racer, joined the podium to speak about a 2017 incident where her midget racer tumbled through the air in an eight-flip wreck at the Petaluma Speedway in northern California[163]. Crone spent the night in the hospital with a concussion and collapsed lung. The next day, she drove herself home, with two black eyes. "I was super fortunate to not get that injured in that good of a wreck," she said.

The fact that Hinchcliffe, Servia, Lindberg and Crone all not only survived their wrecks, but walked away largely unhurt, illustrates the growth and progress made by the motorsports industry over the years.

Still, accidents are serious. A canopy in open-wheel cars may be the next step. IndyCar flirted with the idea of a protective canopy for years, spurred on by two tragedies that shook the series and the racing world to their cores. In 2011, the first, a 15-car pileup at the Las Vegas Motor Speedway, sent thousands of car parts into the air at a high-speed corner. Dan Wheldon, a 33-year old British driver nicknamed "Lionheart," careened toward the crash and slammed his brakes. There was nothing he could do. In a fraction of a second the car slowed from 225 mph to 165 mph to lessen the impact.[164] It didn't matter. Wheldon, who was extremely popular in drivers' circles, plowed into the wreckage and was launched into the air. His helmet was struck—twice. It's unclear what hit him the first time; the second time, video shows, as he twirled off of a catch fence designed to keep him on the track, it was a pole.

In racing we talk about G-forces often. G-force refers to the force of gravity that racecars enact on the body. IndyCar places small sensors called accelerometers all over the cars to measure the forces enacted on the machines and drivers—there are even G-force sensors placed in driver earpieces[165]. A road car that can exceed 1.0G during cornering is considered extremely high performance. Racing drivers will often fight 4 to 5G forces as they dive into turns, which is like strapping 50-pound weights to your head and hanging them off to one side. In the fatal crash, Dan Wheldon experienced three separate head strikes in excess of 110G. The largest was 250G[166]. It was the first IndyCar death in five years and the first in-race death since 1999. Wheldon had won the Indianapolis 500 just weeks earlier, his second. He left a wife, Susie, and one-year old son.

IndyCar vowed to explore all possible safety scenarios. The next season they launched a new body style that had been in development for some time. (Wheldon had provided key input and testing—it would carry the name DW12 for the duration of its use.) The seat and headrest were made more accommodating and supportive; rear bumpers were added to keep car's wheels from touching[167]. The series also seriously considered adding a canopy, but the technology didn't exist to make it feasible. Everything the series' engineers tried was too flimsy, too expensive or too difficult to shape.

It wasn't long before another tragedy shook the series four years later. In 2015, on lap 180 out of 200 at the ABC Supply 500 at Pocono Raceway, the race-leader Sage Karam careened into the wall and sent debris high into the air. Pocono, known as the "Tricky Triangle" for its odd shape and high speeds, had been the site of many crashes before. This one seemed like it would be harmless.

But to avoid hitting Karam's car, James Jakes braked hard. This caused the driver behind him, 37-year old Justin Wilson, to quickly scoot around to the outside of the track. It put him directly in the path of the airborne parts. The force of Karam's accident had sent the front end of his car, known as the nose cone, spinning up and directly down onto Wilson's helmet as he drove by. Wilson had slowed but was still traveling well into triple-digit speeds. For weight balance purposes, the nose cone carries 26 pounds of lead[168]. It landed directly on top of Wilson. He died the next day.

IndyCar had already re-started its effort to build a protective canopy, but Wilson's death brought the issue to national headlines. Within days, according to Jeff Horton, head of protection development at IndyCar, the series received a call from PPG Aerospace, a supplier of military-grade materials. "We think we can help you," the company told Horton, who relayed the story at the safety seminar.

"Having a partner like this is unbelievable," Horton said. As it turns out, PPG Aerospace had previous experience with impact resistance in high-pressure environments. The company makes canopies and windscreens for military aircraft such as the F-15, F-16, B-1 Lancer and B-52 Stratofortress bombers. Its canopies—"They call them 'transparencies,'" Horton said—are designed to withstand a 35-pound concrete cinderblock dropped onto a train moving 70 mph.

PPG offered IndyCar transparencies from the F-16 that had been broken in testing to sample. Horton and his team jumped at the opportunity, learning to shape and fit the ultra-strength material to a racecar. They tested several materials for a new canopy including polycarbonate, stretched acrylic and Opticor—the last, a synthetic material developed internally by PPG[169]. In the end, Indycar selected Opticor for its strength, weight, flexibility and fire resistance. It performed better than the others on an abrasion resistance test. Some drivers expressed concerns: from cleanliness and sunlight glare to visual distortion due to the curvature. But sitting inside the car, Horton says, it's almost impossible to tell there is any canopy present at all. Driving tests on a virtual simulator revealed positive feedback from several drivers.

It's already been tested in the real world, in several sessions run by four-time IndyCar champion Scott Dixon at IMS Speedway near Phoenix[170]. Vision wasn't the problem, Dixon said. The biggest issues are the lack of airflow that drivers have spent their entire lives growing accustomed to, he said. That, and the silence. But these are minor issues in the grand scheme. Horton believes if the transparency had been fitted to Justin Wilson's car it could have saved his life. “If we can bless this, load-wise, we’ll put it on as soon as we can,” Horton told the crowd in Long Beach.

Personal safety isn’t a traditional point of pride in the motorsports world, but instead, more like a happy accident. Since the early days of racing, glamorized especially in the fast-and-loose 1960s, the racer mentality has been that of the dashing daredevil staring death in the face and laughing. They put themselves in extreme risk, sometimes stubbornly so. Many wore the number of funerals they attended as a badge of honor and decried safety advancements as a softening of the sport that moved racing away from its core principles.

The difference now, said Julia Daly, a head trauma specialist at Sargent College, is that we know better.

“What is a concussion?” Daly asked the seminar crowd. “Do you have to hit your head? Do you have to lose consciousness?” The answer to both is no. A concussion, she explained, is simply a brain injury. In a race car, there is catastrophic risk around every corner, but the seemingly mundane can be an issue as well. Drivers can sustain a concussion simply by spinning out at a high speed—even if the car doesn’t make contact with anything, just the whipping around is enough to jostle the brain. Fewer than 10 percent of concussions result in a blackout, and they aren’t independent of one another. The cumulative effect of many small collisions, even knocking your helmet against the roll cage, over the course of a racing career can add up to damaging results.

This level of information simply wasn’t available during the heyday of the “tough-guy” racecar driver and only started trickling in as late as the 1990s. Only since about 2000 has racing truly begun to grapple with its concussion risk, Daly said. The tough guy mentality is similar to the one that has plagued professional football in recent years, with the National Football League struggling to adapt from the common practice of players remaining in the game through pain and injury. The NFL’s new concussion protocol has gone through a rocky implementation phase that still isn’t held in high medical regard.

Safety efforts have been an uphill climb in racing too. After the 2001 crash that killed Dale Earnhardt, one of the most popular and decorated racers in NASCAR history, drivers refused to adopt the HANS neck support device[171] that many believe would have saved Earnhardt's life. NASCAR didn't give them a choice, mandating the use of HANS later in the season. Today no professional driver is allowed to race without a HANS device, even in amateur motorsports. Safety rules for the 24 Hours of LeMons junkyard series requires some kind of head and neck restraint system. Series are also doing a better job of providing medical attention before, during and after cars are on the track.

"We have a lot more support in the world of racing today than we ever have," St. James told me. "One of the things that used to drive me fricking crazy is I knew how much support was available to other athletes. They had incredible staffs of medical people to help them with massage therapy and training and injury prevention. All we had was a medical center if you got in a crash. It was very, 'You figure it out,' and I thought that was awful that our sport didn't provide that level of infrastructure."

Equally as important, St. James said, is that experts like Daly, the brain trauma specialist, are finally being heard by the organizers.

"I think we've caught up a bit now. Almost every professional team has their massage therapist and workout equipment. Information being available to teams and drivers has finally caught up, including concussion studies. I think there was such a fear for the industry to even go down this path for fear of legal action. All I know is finally Pandora's Box has been opened and now every driver has trainers. It's now much better."

More research is being done to continue to improve safety conditions for everyone on the track. Medical teams learned, for instance, that transporting drivers on stabilizer boards to decrease the risk of spinal injury can actually cause unnecessary spinal movement. In many cases it's better to instruct the driver to self-stabilize, said Joe Powell, an emergency paramedic experienced in track safety and rescue. Stabilizer boards also decrease the flow of blood to the brain. Powell estimates that the use of stabilizer boards will be phased out of motorsports in the next 5 to 7 years. He also said the habit drilled into paramedics to immediately administer fluids via an IV puts the patient at risk of high blood pressure that causes excessive bleeding.

"Why do we do it? Because we've been doing it for the last 30 years," Powell said.

Many facilities are installing softer walls around the raceway to lessen the impact of a collision. Series officials are also considering more widespread availability of an experimental drug called tranexamic acid, or TXA. In a major trauma, like a racing collision, administering TXA can prevent blood loss and manage proper, healthy blood clotting. A paper set to be published by Powell and other experts in the journal *Annals of Behavioral Medicine* explained that the earlier TXA is delivered the better. The researchers found that TXA improves the 28-day mortality rate by 57 percent. The drug was approved for paramedic use throughout California just weeks before Powell spoke to the crowd during the seminar. It was not available for the race in Long Beach that continued outside the seminar doors, though it may not be long before TXA is a fixture in IndyCar and other series. It addresses one of many dangers facing the motorsports community that people like Powell are racing to solve.

"What's the moonshot?" Powell said. "I think it's whether we can slow the deceleration of the brain inside the skull. You're not going to stop the brain from bouncing around. So how do you decrease the deceleration? I don't have the answer to that. But I think we all believe there's a way to do it. And one day we'll figure it out."

Chapter XIV: Roots

Eighty miles west of Los Angeles, in the farming community of Oxnard, between a small municipal airport and a strawberry field, on the second story of a nondescript industrial building, there is a set of doors. Two of them, side by side, brown and tan with a gaping circular hole in the middle. They stand more than seven feet tall and nearly five feet wide, set into a display wall for visitors to observe. The bottom half is covered in butterscotch-colored vellum. The area surrounding the circle is deep brown Italian walnut carved into intricate patterns and shapes. Glowing accent pieces are made of copper. The doors are striking from a distance and remarkable up close. They once served as the entryway to the birthplace of the most beautiful cars ever made.

The doors were built by Carlo Bugatti, a Milan-born designer and craftsman, in or around 1885. Bugatti trained in architecture[172], specialized in Art Nouveau furniture and dabbled in jewelry and musical instruments. Fame took Bugatti outside Italy. He frequently traveled to France and established multiple ateliers in both countries. Bugatti had two sons, Ettore and Rembrandt. The first became a heralded engineer; the second an emotive sculptor. When Ettore founded a car company, Automobiles E. Bugatti, in 1909, the doors built by his father were brought to headquarters in Alsace, France. They were installed in the entrance to the drawing room.

As children, Ettore and Rembrandt grew up assisting their father in his workshop. They watched him sketch and shape, then sanded and stretched at his direction. By the time Ettore turned 23, his dad had moved to Paris and won international acclaim for his imaginative furniture that was at once asymmetrical, awkward and amalgamated of several conflicting influences. As striking and strange as they were, from his tables and drawers to his desks and nightstands, Carlo's works followed a consistent design language and theme. They were different, but they still fit together. They set a mood. And they were always, unfailingly, exquisitely built.

Ettore, the eldest, followed his father's creative footsteps. From the beginning, his company made its mark on the car world. Early models featured engines hand built by Ettore, whose engineering skills at the time were unparalleled. Introduced in 1909, Bugatti cars were instantly the fastest on the road. Over time they became the fastest cars on the track. A Bugatti won the first-ever Grand Prix of Monaco in 1929—they qualified in five of the top six positions and finished in six of the top seven. Bugattis won the Mille Miglia, Carrera Panamerica and the 24 Hours of Le Mans. The company experimented with advancements in suspension, aerodynamics, cooling and other components while competitors were simply trying to match their speed. Bugattis of the time were styled in bold colors with wild hood scoops, fender flares and bracing bars. They were exorbitant. They were irresistible. Each one wore a horseshoe-shaped front grille and bright red oval badge with the word "BUGATTI" across it.

Bugatti stamped its legend in 1924, when it debuted the Type 35, a racecar for the road with a teardrop rear end that would set the standard for the next century of motorsport design. It worked exceptionally well. The Type 35 won more than 2,000 races around the world. Twelve years after its debut, the company changed the course of automotive history again. Ettore enlisted the help of his own son, Jean Bugatti, and tasked him with bringing a rule-breaking supercar to life. It would be based on the 1935 Bugatti Aerolithe, a stunning concept sport version of the 1934 Type 57 that Jean also designed. The Aerolithe combined the traditional long Bugatti hood with dramatic fenders, covered rear wheels, suicide doors and a sloping roofline that ended in a boat-like tail. It also had a central fin stretching from end to end. To save weight, the Aerolithe was made of magnesium, an extremely light metal. But magnesium can't be welded, so the central fin held the two twin sides of the body together with rivets.

Jean Bugatti set to taking the Aerolithe from concept to production model, based on the popular Bugatti Type 57 touring car. He took the lowered racing body of the Type 57S and matched it with the supercharged engine in the Type 57C[173], making it an SC. He called it the 57SC Atlantic. The 57SC Atlantic represented the absolute pinnacle of the Bugatti philosophy at the height of its powers. It took everything the company knew about materials, weight savings, chassis tech, racing prowess and engine advancements and wrapped it in a quintessential Art Deco design by Jean Bugatti, designed in the shadow of the vellum and walnut doors made by his grandfather. The Bugatti 57SC Atlantic must be the most striking vehicle ever built. Only four were made. One was lost[174]. One was hit by a train[175]. One belongs to Ralph Lauren. And I'm standing in front of the other one.

*

The light blue 1936 Bugatti 57SC Atlantic is housed in the Mullin Automotive Museum, a nonprofit[176] museum located in Oxnard since 2010. It's open to the public, who can tour a vast and impressive car collection that also includes the doors built by Carlo Bugatti, as well as his furniture and his son Rembrandt's animal sculptures. There are dozens of Bugattis inside, several of which competed in and won races across Europe. Others have won prestigious show awards. One sat at the bottom of a lake in France for 75 years before being dragged to the surface and flown to an office park next to a strawberry field in Oxnard. The museum also includes a dazzling collection of pre-war classics from Delahaye, Avions Voisin, Talbot Lago and more. Walking the halls is like gazing into the minds of people who were only beginning to figure out the inner workings of cars, how to extract their performance and develop their shapes. Some of the cars, like the Atlantic, really work. Others—like a 1922 Renault Type JV limousine with a horizontally-mounted radiator at the base of an extremely long Gonzo nose—definitely don't.

Each vehicle at the Mullin is capable of fetching huge sums on the open market. A maroon Talbot-Lago Type 150-C-S, also in the running for most beautiful car ever built, had a similar model sell for the U.S. equivalent of $4 million in 2017[177]. Rumor has it the Mullin paid $40 million for its Atlantic. The crazy thing about visiting the museum is that, unlike many others, the cars are not behind ropes. There are no enclosed cases or glass walls. There are no guards roaming around to make sure your hands stay in your pockets. At one point I found myself completely alone in a small dark room with the half-rotted husk of the Bugatti Type 22 that spent 75 years underwater. As a visitor to the Mullin, you're free to roam where you please, strolling between millions of dollars worth of fenders without worry. It makes a bygone era of supercars accessible to anyone with $30. Even the annual membership, which includes access to an on-site dining room and scheduled field trips to Jay Leno's private garage in the San Fernando Valley, is a reasonable $85.

I asked my docent, a tall and jolly man in a newsie cap named Greg Hayward, what ties all the cars together. He explained that every car in the collection went underappreciated in its time. In the early 1900s, until the beginning of World War II, the general public was still growing accustomed to a life with cars. Automakers often had no idea whether they would be around another year, and essentially existed model to model. Nobody, not the owners, the drivers, the admirers or even the builders, realized what they had.

"They were all taken for granted," Hayward told me. While these cars were laying the foundations of car design and performance, setting speed records and redefining the car's place in modern society, they were also regularly being abused and neglected. Several of the cars on display at the Mullin were rescued from barns. The purpose of the Mullin is to spread appreciation of these cars now, to understand the barriers that were broken and how these milestones helped us get to where we are today.

I wandered the halls of the Mullin, passing one legendary model after another, all time capsules of engineering and creativity. Back then, there was no blueprint. Every progression, advancement and improvement in those days was a minor miracle.

"Everything was an experiment, pretty much," Hayward said. Engine power came relatively quickly, but it took a while for the rest of the car to catch up. At first, high-performance cars had very little high-speed stability, so automakers made their fastest cars out of heavy-duty frames. But that made them too rigid to turn, so they added hand brakes mounted externally to the outside of the car and pulled them to drift around corners. When the cars needed better balance they pushed the engine away from the front and toward the driver—a few inches at first. When they needed to shed a few pounds, they experimented with lighter weight materials: steel, aluminum and magnesium, which led to the famous rivets in the Bugatti 57SC Atlantic. It would later lead to the space-age carbon fiber chassis we have today.

Car companies needed to innovate on a yearly basis back then—or risk going out of business. The old adage "Race on Sunday, sell on Monday" was never more true than it was then. Every vehicle built needed to sell in order to recuperate its design and production cost. The best way to sell cars was to win races, which in those days were a huge deal. Automakers poured everything they had into every vehicle, often spending resources on design, research and development down to the last dollar. This was true in the luxury world, too. Cars featured dramatic curves, boat-tails, tidal wave fenders and luxurious amenities. In the Mullin, one Hispano-Suiza featured a body hand-built with oak and mahogany. A 1928 Citroen B14 Coupe wore a geometric paint scheme designed by Art Deco master Sonia Delaunay that debuted at a Paris art show alongside two models wearing matching dresses.

"There was a total disregard for budget and a total dedication to beauty," Hayward said. "There was no thought given to, 'How do we do this again?'"

In this do-or-die environment it may be a surprise to learn that competitors were also willing to share with one another. Car companies often made their patents publicly available and openly discussed their progress with others. The car was not only a business investment; it was a tool to advance the betterment of mankind. The automotive industry fundamentally changed the course of human travel. It expanded the delivery and shipping of goods. It altered the design of major cities, made new jobs available to people in rural locations and advanced the possibilities of exploration. The chance to improve the car was seen as a chance to leave your mark on world history.

This may seem an overly self-important tag to place on companies essentially building exorbitant vanity projects for overstuffed collectors to store away like Fabergé eggs. But it is genuinely how automakers saw themselves, Hayward said, and they often worked together with their closest competitors so that mass transportation could one day reach more people.

It's a stark contrast to today's automotive industry, in which decisions are often made not by visionaries and boundary-pushing dreamers but by accounting departments and day traders. The extent to which boards of directors have increased their influence over the operation of car companies has done more damage to automotive progress, and arguably society, than simply slowing the development of racecars or canceling interesting designs.

Automakers are governed today by their shareholders, who expect not just quarterly returns but *ever-increasing* returns, which makes the companies vulnerable to cost-cutting measures that diminish the quality of the products. One bad statement can cost thousands of assembly line jobs in order to salvage shareholder profits. Modern car companies long ago stopped working toward a common societal good. The most egregious example may be the industry's continued lobbying of Congress to roll back the fuel economy standards required by the Environmental Protection Agency. By all accounts, the industry currently possesses the technology necessary to exceed those very standards and decrease global emissions on a massive scale moving forward. But the industry is handicapping itself in the name of money, when it should be pushing the boundaries of efficiency instead.

The one exception to this trend, it can be argued, is Tesla Motors. The company and its visionary chief executive, Elon Musk, have not only steadfastly adhered to the goal of an emissions-free future but invested in research and development and pioneered technology to bring society closer to that reality on a scale that dozens of companies ten times their size do not dare approach. Tesla shattered the barrier that automakers routinely trotted out to justify their disinterest in developing electric cars: that the car-buying public is not interested in going electric. Today this is demonstrably untrue, in large part due to Tesla. The company has also established its own network of charging station infrastructure. It's expanded the potential of a culture that runs increased amounts of its power off an electric grid.

The story of Tesla cannot be told without its faults. It rushed into autonomous technology and marketed it in a way that put its own customers in danger. Musk makes bombastic statements and predictions that lead to rushed deadlines, wayward workplace safety standards and a Ponzi-style fundraising model. And his lasseiz-faire attitude toward financial reporting and disclosure gambles with the investments—and in many cases, retirement plans—of everyday people.

But automotive history is littered with Elon Musks. Many of them were so eccentric they make Musk look like a choir teacher in comparison. The real shift did not come from the arrival of Elon Musk but the departure of visionaries like him from the automotive industry. It was once a business filled with dreamers who would have taken the opportunity Musk provided and used it to advance technology and expand markets whether it paid immediate financial dividends or not. These were people who thought about the generations that would come after them, and what they could do now to make new things possible then. The lack of such an environment in contemporary business means that Tesla has instead been left to shoulder the heavy lifting itself. Today, luxury companies such as Porsche, Mercedes-Benz and Jaguar Land Rover are beginning to take initial steps toward providing a true challenge in the electric market. (In some cases, as with Volkswagen, they're going electric only after public environmental scandals dragged them into such a commitment kicking and screaming.)

This is not to say that large companies will cease inventing and innovating. There is vast opportunity for automakers to continue to improve the vehicles we drive every day, whether that means developing environmentally-responsible methods or extracting every ounce of performance possible. There are passionate engineers and designers at every car company in the world working hard to make products that enhance and enrich peoples' lives. But the more I learn about automotive history—and the more I spend time with people today who are not only enthusiastic about cars but have adjusted their lives to fit around their passion—the more I believe automotive innovations and progress will be driven by individuals on the front lines of car culture before it is driven by billion-dollar global conglomerates. The mind of Ettore Bugatti came up with the idea to rake the angle of a windscreen to better slice through the air. Other racing marques adopted the idea and it became widespread. When American soldiers in Europe caught sight of the dramatic angle, they returned to U.S. shores and took saws to the roofs of their Ford Model As, creating the chopped effect that would eventually lead to the hot rod era. Only then did U.S. designers in major design studios begin to take notice.

Were there people back then who criticized the raked-screen Bugattis? Did they mock U.S. teens or cry blasphemy as they desecrated their Model As? Were there those who warned of the dangers of hot rodding and claimed it marked the end of automotive culture? I'm sure of it, just as there are those who lambasted lowriders, donks and drifting after them, and just as there are people who can't stand the sight of stanced suspensions, time-attack wings and spoilers and safari Porsches today.

The greatest myth about car culture is that it has ever been a single style or idea. Car culture by its very nature is fluid and ever-changing, stopping only long enough to influence the next generation of builders and racers. The only thing you accomplish by decrying homegrown automotive trends is making yourself irrelevant. You give ammunition to people like Malcolm Gladwell, who so disdained current car culture that he didn't bother to see it for himself. By participating and celebrating, instead, you give yourself the opportunity to help shape it. When you stop pining for the past, you find the chance to influence the future.

So what cars will be the new classics? What are the cars rolling off assembly lines today that will one day inspire a new generation of enthusiasts, engineers, designers and racers? Is it hypercars like the Senna, a pinnacle of modern performance without regard to cost? Is it sports cars like the 911 R, a return to purity of function and form? Is it aesthetic landmarks like the Audi A7 or BMW 6-Series Gran Coupe? Is it factory juice like the Honda Civic Type R, a very fast version of a very slow car? Part of the reason it's difficult to guess what will resonate with future generations is we don't know what they will value, but looking to the past provides clues. In the pre-war era, the cars with lasting legacies earned them through innovation, beauty, bespoke construction and racing heritage. The same criteria hold true, for the most part, through the muscle car and Radwood eras. Looking at the cars of today, there are only a few models that stand out with a chance to make a real mark on the culture of tomorrow.

In my opinion, the rise of the performance four-door "coupe" combines size, beauty and speed in unique ways. Vehicles like the Audi RS7 and, on the value side, Kia Stinger come to mind. In terms of pure performance and enjoyment, the Porsche Cayman GT4 and Lotus Evora are hard to beat. Strictly aesthetically, the Lexus LC500, Aston Martin DBS and Volvo V90 station wagon seem to set new bars for design. The hypercars and sports cars that will drive automotive enthusiasm into the future are easy to identify. The tougher challenge is predicting which cars will be accessible and affordable. In the past these have been models like the E30 M3, the Nissan Silvia, the Toyota Supra—cars that can be had for a reasonable price, provide the baseline performance and parts availability to support a healthy aftermarket. Today, though, the modern versions of those cars are out of reach for most. What that leaves is pony cars—the Mustang, Camaro and Challenger—and a handful of foreign models like the Subaru Impreza, Mitsubishi Evo and Hyundai Genesis coupe. And then there are the ones that embody "slow car fast"—the Civic Type R, Focus RS and BMW 1M. Maybe a dark horse or two will stumble into building a fanbase like the short-lived Cadillac ATS or Chevrolet SS. The supercars and hypercars inspire, but a healthy car culture has access to capable and available vehicles that are easy to upgrade and tune. When the future equivalent of Radwood comes to celebrate cars of the 2000s and 2010s, already coined hilariously as "Litwood" by *Jalopnik* editor-in-chief Patrick George, these could be the kinds of cars that grace the lots.

The writing is on the wall when it comes to the future of the automobile. Electrification is no longer a passing fancy nor a pesky requirement that can be fulfilled and then shelved. Hybrid and battery-electric cars are here and will show the way to a sustainable tomorrow. Car culture will be no different.

The world of cars continues to evolve and change, and young enthusiasts who are coming into the hobby now will be inspired by cars using as much juice as they do combustion. They won't view an electric motor as a drawback, but instead as an opportunity. Battery packs and electric motors provide unlimited potential for enthusiasts to upgrade, improve and tune to their unique desires and needs as they see fit. And when it comes time to build their collections, they'll want the cars that inspired that love in the first place. On the supercar side, there are obvious contenders. The plug-in 2013

McLaren P1 will prove to be the most coveted car in that automaker's history after the F1. The plug-in 2014 Porsche 918 is arguably the most groundbreaking car the company made in decades. The BMW i8 has a real chance to become a future darling due to its daring looks, futuristic hybrid powertrain and relative value. The Volkswagen e-Golf wins the hearts and minds of virtually anyone who drives it. We also need to have a national conversation about Tesla and its super-high performance P100D models.

What's clear about the electric future is that its adoption does not spell the end of driving fun. Hybrid and electric cars will continue to influence the progression of both efficiency and performance. We will begin to think about what performance means in new ways. Maybe, a few years from now, every car will be capable of zero-60 runs in four seconds or less. So then what does it mean to have a fast car? Maybe we can manipulate the energy to create power at different times to increase feedback and responsiveness. Maybe we can direct that power to modulate between better mileage or power depending on driving conditions. Maybe we will find some unforeseen way to use electricity to our advantage as enthusiasts, rather than as an impediment. Whatever the case, electric power in cars is here to stay.

The rise of automated and autonomous driving in recent years, while making an intriguing case for improved safety that could potentially save millions of lives, also made promises it does not seem will be achievable within a timeline of several decades. It is batteries and electric motors, not Level 5 self-driving vehicles, that will shape the future of cars and personal transportation. They will enable us as a society to finally confront our role in choking the planet and help us find solutions to make it re-inhabitable one day. They will create discourse about sustainability, alternative power grids and efficiency of movement. They will re-define the way we think about cars.

*

The lesson the all-star collection at the Mullin Museum teaches us is that cars that embody true innovation and dedication to craft will never die. Cars that, even if misguided or flawed or labeled as spectacular failures of their time, try to move the culture forward are going to have a place in the world. When we look back on the history of car culture, these cars will have carved out a permanent niche for themselves. It's why a 1911 Hispano-Suiza is enshrined for pushing its engine back a few inches. It's why someone paid $7.3 million for a Peugeot that never won a race. It's why people still salivate over the DeLorean, a stainless-steel wedge of cheese that can barely hit 100 mph. Following trends and maintaining the status quo is a great way to fill coffers and keep shareholders fat and happy. True innovation, real artistry, a true mission to serve the betterment of mankind—these are the qualities that create legends.

Even if companies continue to be driven by their boardrooms, there will always be people that take what they were given and create something great. There will always be the people: the influencers, the enthusiasts, the organizers and connectors. There will always be meets and shows and rallies and auctions. There will always be these epicenters, even if they're virtual, for automotive enthusiasts to gather, share, argue and inspire. They keep Brionna Lynch in search of the perfect chassis for her dream 2JZ motor. They inspire Matt Farah to slap some mud tires on a Porsche 911 and tear through the forest. They convince Seely clients to open their checkbooks for another chance to own an instant classic. The automotive industry needs dreamers and visionaries now more than ever. They are the ones we will remember. They are the ones that will attract new enthusiasts to keep the culture moving forward. Automotive enthusiasm will change. It has to. But it isn't going anywhere.

I stared into the deep purple paint of the Talbot-Lago T150-C SS for a long time. The car is 80 years old and looks like it's from 80 years in the future. It is difficult to express how deep the wheelwells swoop and dive. There are cooling vents and louvres that make it feel like you're peering into the car's soul. As you move around the car, its shape shifts and transforms. You become wind, finding creases and crevices to send your vision flowing over its bodywork. I felt the urge to hug it. The car came to be when Italian businessman Antonio Lago bought Automobiles Talbot in 1936[178]. Lago was a talented engineer who developed the six-cylinder engine in the T150-C SS. But Lago did not simply want to build a fast car. His magic was realizing he needed help.

Lago hired an assortment of specialists, bringing in top experts when it came to suspension, braking, balance, handling and of course design. This was rare in those days. Most owners of automobile companies, like the Bugattis, were eccentric, extremely hands-on micro-managers who insisted on involvement in every step of the process. Lago was different. He helmed the creation of a masterpiece that started with a good frame and stunning design. Then it got the race-proven engine, which earned it the T150-C, or competizione, designation. Then it got a short wheelbase for better handling, lending it the SS, or super sports, badge[179]. And now it was parked at my feet. I was staring at one of the first slow cars fast.

Hearing Hayward tell the Lago's story, and now absorbing the car through my eyes, trying to make sense of what it took in those days to create something so stunning, I thought of something I'd heard months earlier. It was while sitting in Joey Seely's car, Project Nasty, the engine screaming behind us, as he espoused his beliefs in the minutiae of handling and balance. He talked about the car, his pride and joy, recounting all the small projects that amounted to the fine-tuned machine around us.

I stopped him and asked for his motivation, what drove him to keep tuning when it seemed good enough. What drove him to improve when so many admired what he had already accomplished. What drove him to keep coming back. He turned to me with a look that suggested I hadn't listed to a single word he'd been saying all day.

"That's what I do," he said. "I make grip."

He whipped the gated transmission shifter from fourth gear down to third and stepped on the gas. He yelled over the frenzy of the engine.

"This is fun!" he shouted. "Too many people take all the fun out of it!"

Bibliography

The following books were helpful to me:

Taylor, James. *BMW M3: The Complete Story*. The Crowood Press, 2014.

Gross, Ken. *So-Cal Coupe*. Stance & Speed, 2013.

Scalzo, Joe. *City of Speed: Los Angeles and the Rise of American Racing*. Motorbooks, 2007.

About the Author

Ryan ZumMallen is Reviews Editor with Edmunds.com and an automotive journalist with more than 10 years of experience. His work has appeared in *Road & Track*, *Car And Driver*, *The Verge*, *Autoweek*, *Autobytel and Trucks.com.* He graduated from California State University at Long Beach and has been a reporter ever since. Slow Car Fast is his first book.

Carrara Media, LLC
To learn more about Carrara Media and its products, events and newsletters, visit CarraraBooks.com.

Citations

[1] Collin Woodard, Brian Silvestro and Chris Perkins, "17 of the Fastest Four-Doors Around the Nurburgring," *RoadAndTrack.com*, June 13, 2019, https://www.roadandtrack.com/car-culture/g6778/suv-hatchback-sedan-nurburgring-lap/?slide=8.

[2] Máté Petrány, "When Ayrton Senna Had A Joke On Williams And Sonic The Hedgehog," *Jalopnik.com*, May 1, 2016, https://jalopnik.com/when-ayrton-senna-had-a-joke-on-williams-and-sonic-the-1774114277.

[3] "Porsche 959," *Wikipedia.com*, https://en.wikipedia.org/wiki/Porsche_959.

[4] Dennis Simanaitis, "First Look Flashback: 1987 Ferrari F40," *RoadAndTrack.com*, July 21, 2017, https://www.roadandtrack.com/new-cars/first-drives/reviews/a25595/first-look-flashback-1987-ferrari-f40/.

[5] "Production Car Speed Record," *Wikipedia.com*, https://en.wikipedia.org/wiki/Production_car_speed_record.

[6] Max Prince, "5 Things You Didn't Know About the Lamborghini Countach," *TheDrive.com*, September 19, 2016, https://www.thedrive.com/vintage/5226/5-things-you-didnt-know-about-the-lamborghini-countach.

[7] Chris Shunk, "TomTom data reveals U.S. drivers' average speed, fastest highway," *Autoblog.com*, January 26, 2010, https://www.autoblog.com/2010/01/26/tomtom-data-reveals-u-s-drivers-average-speed-fastest-highway/.

[8] Chris Perkins, "Here's Every New Car On Sale That Goes 200 MPH or Faster," *RoadAndTrack.com*, February 11, 2019, https://www.roadandtrack.com/new-cars/g10290437/fastest-new-cars/.

[9] "Ford Mustang: A Brief History in Zero-to-60-MPH Acceleration," *CarAndDriver.com*, February 7, 2018, https://www.caranddriver.com/features/g15105913/ford-mustang-gt-0-60-times.

[10] Kyle Stock and David Ingold, "America's Cars Are Suddenly Getting Faster and More Efficient," *Bloomberg.com*, May 17, 2017, https://www.bloomberg.com/news/features/2017-05-17/america-s-cars-are-all-fast-and-furious-these-days.

[11] "Toyota 0-60 MPH Times," *Zeroto60times.com*, https://www.zeroto60times.com/vehicle-make/toyota-0-60-mph-times/.

[12] "Lightning Lap Results 2006 to 2018: Every Car, Every Lap Time," *CarAndDriver.com*, September 19, 2018, https://www.caranddriver.com/features/a23319884/lightning-lap-times-historical-data/ - sidepanel.

[13] "Nurburgring is the Be-All End-All for Auto-Manufacturer Testing," *Autoweek.com*, September 17, 2015, https://autoweek.com/article/car-news/nurburgring-be-all-end-all-auto-manufacturer-testing.

[14] "Nordschleife," *FastestLaps.com*, https://fastestlaps.com/tracks/nordschleife.

[15] Brian Silvestro, "The 2019 Mercedes-AMG GLC63 S Is the Quickest SUV Ever at the Nurburgring," *RoadAndTrack.com*, November 26, 2018, https://www.roadandtrack.com/new-cars/a25304679/2019-mercedes-amg-glc63-s-nurburgring-lap-record/.

[16] Chris Perkins, "Alfa Romeo Giulia Beats Porsche Panamera Turbo as Fastest Sedan at the 'Ring," *RoadAndTrack.com*, September 8, 2016, https://www.roadandtrack.com/new-cars/news/a30714/alfa-romeo-giulia-nurburgring-lap-time/.

[17] Travis Okulski, "The 500 Horsepower, Manual-Only, Lightweight 911R Is the Porsche of Your Dreams," *RoadAndTrack.com*, March 1, 2016, https://www.roadandtrack.com/car-shows/geneva-auto-show/news/a28335/porsche-911-r-revealed/.

[18] Justin T. Westbrook, "How the Mighty Have Fallen: 30-Mile Porsche 911 R Estimated to Take Measly $375,000 at Auction," *Jalopnik.com*, August 14, 2018, https://jalopnik.com/how-the-mighty-have-fallen-30-mile-porsche-911-r-estim-1828342821.

[19] Michael Sivak and Brandon Schoettle, "Recent Decreases in the Proportion of Persons with a Driver's License across All Age Groups," The University of Michigan Transportation Research Institute, January 2016, http://www.umich.edu/~umtriswt/PDF/UMTRI-2016-4_Abstract_English.pdf.

[20] Jay Serafino, "New Guidelines Redefine Birth Years for Millennials, Gen-X, and 'Post-Millennials'," *MentalFloss.com*, March 1, 2018, http://mentalfloss.com/article/533632/new-guidelines-redefine-birth-years-millennials-gen-x-and-post-millennials.

[21] Richard Fry, "Millennials projected to overtake Baby Boomers as America's largest generation," *PewResearch.org*, March 1, 2018, http://www.pewresearch.org/fact-tank/2018/03/01/millennials-overtake-baby-boomers/.

[22] Alexandre Tanzi, "Millennials Are Facing $1 Trillion in Debt," *Bloomberg.com*, February 25, 2019, https://www.bloomberg.com/news/articles/2019-02-25/millennials-face-1-trillion-debt-as-student-loans-pile-up.

[23] "The Recession of 2007–2009," Bureau of Labor Statistics, February 2012, https://www.bls.gov/spotlight/2012/recession/pdf/recession_bls_spotlight.pdf.

[24] "Millennials earn 20% less than Boomers did at same stage of life," *USAToday.com*, January 13, 2017, https://www.usatoday.com/story/money/2017/01/13/millennials-falling-behind-boomer-parents/96530338/.

[25] "Auto•No•Mo'•Us: Addressing the Totality of the Driverless Car," *CarAndDriver.com*, October 3, 2017, https://www.caranddriver.com/features/a15079838/autonomous-addressing-the-totality-of-the-driverless-car-feature/.

[26] Tom Vanderbilt, "Autonomous Cars: How Safe Is Safe Enough?," *CarAndDriver.com*, October 3, 2017, https://www.caranddriver.com/features/a15080598/autonomous-cars-how-safe-is-safe-enough-feature/.

[27] "Why Today's Teens Are More Depressed Than Ever," *CenterForDiscovery.com*, https://centerfordiscovery.com/blog/todays-teens-depressed-ever/.

[28] Joe Lynch, "Check Out These Surprising Stats About U.S. Music Festivals," *Billboard.com*, April 22, 2015, https://www.billboard.com/articles/columns/music-festivals/6539009/music-festival-statistics-graphic.

[29] "More Americans of all ages spurning driver's licenses," *UMTRI.UMich.edu*, January 20, 2016, http://www.umtri.umich.edu/what-were-doing/news/more-americans-all-ages-spurning-drivers-licenses.

[30] "2006 Long Beach Grand Prix - Events," *SuperStreetOnline.com*, February 17, 2009, http://www.superstreetonline.com/event-coverage/motorsports/0609-epcp-2006-long-beach-grand-prix/.

[31] Caleb Jacobs, "Long Beach Grand Prix Attendance Highest in 18 Years," *TheDrive.com*, April 19, 2018, http://www.thedrive.com/accelerator/20259/long-beach-grand-prix-attendance-highest-in-18-years.

[32] "Spotter's Guide: Grand Prix of Long Beach 2018," Pirelli World Challenge, http://files.world-challenge.com/events/2018-04-lbgp/2018-PWC-LBGP-SpottersGuide.pdf.

[33] David Cole, "Los Angeles Karting Championship Ends Summer with Round Seven," EKartingNews.com, August 29, 2018, https://ekartingnews.com/2018/08/29/los-angeles-karting-championship-ends-summer-with-round-seven/.

[34] "Piotr Wiecek Claims Double Victory in Motegi Super Drift Weekend," *FormulaD.com*, April 16, 2018, http://news.formulad.com/2018/04/page/2/.
[35] "Race Results," IMSA WeatherTech Sports Car Championship, https://sportscarchampionship.imsa.com/schedule-results/current-results?eventid=89&sessid=675.
[36] Gabriel A. Solis, "The Revolutionary History of Lowriders," *Vice.com*, May 10, 2017, http://www.historyaccess.com/historyoflowride.html.
[37] Interview with Brian Nigos, June 24, 2018.
[38] Richard S. Chang, "The Ones Who Started It All," *SuperStreetOnline.com*, July 1, 2000, http://www.superstreetonline.com/features/20325/.
[39] Corey Takahaski, "CAR CULTURE / With its own slang, style and ethos, the import scene is a youth movement with speed to burn," *Newsday.com*, June 20, 2001, https://www.newsday.com/lifestyle/car-culture-with-its-own-slang-style-and-ethos-the-import-scene-is-a-youth-movement-with-speed-to-burn-1.802590.
[40] "Joest Racing," *Wikipedia.com*, https://en.wikipedia.org/wiki/Joest_Racing - Audi_Sport_Team_Joest.
[41] "LuftAuto002 - The Safari Porsche 911," *SuperStreetOnline*, August 2, 2018, http://www.superstreetonline.com/features/1808-luftauto002-the-safari-porsche-911.
[42] "Rywire's Project E-AT - Updating A Classic," *superstreetonline.com*, November 6, 2013, http://www.superstreetonline.com/how-to/chassis-suspension/1310-rywire-project-e-at/.
[43] "A Visit to Matt Farah's Podcast Studio," *Spike's Car Radio*, May 29, 2018.
[44] "1968 Porsche 908 Works 'Short-Tail' Coupe," *RMSothebys.com*, https://rmsothebys.com/en/auctions/MO18/Monterey/lots/r0001-1968-porsche-908-works-short-tail-coupe/641223.
[45] "Lüftgekuhlt 5 - Part 1," *SuperStreetOnline.com*, April 26, 2018, http://www.superstreetonline.com/event-coverage/car-shows/1804-luftgekuhlt-5-part-1/.
[46] Victor Varela, "Luftgekühlt 2018 – Report and Photos," *SportsCarDigest.com*, April 25, 2018, https://www.sportscardigest.com/luftgekuhlt-2018-report-photos/4/?envira_id=278848 - envira-gallery-wrap-278848.
[47] Chris Cushing, "A Brief History of the 356: Origins," *FlatSixes.com*, February 17, 2017, http://flatsixes.com/cars/porsche-356/history-porsche-356/.
[48] Aaron Severson, "History of the Porsche 911," *Autoweek.com*, December 3, 2013, http://autoweek.com/article/car-life/history-porsche-911.
[49] "Zero F*cks Given 2: The Jettamino," *The Smoking Tire*, February 11, 2014, https://www.youtube.com/watch?v=DPN8kFGNPhc.
[50] "37 Mind Blowing YouTube Facts, Figures and Statistics – 2019," *MerchDope.com*, June 15, 2019, https://merchdope.com/youtube-statistics/.
[51] "You know what's cool? A billion hours," YouTube.GoogleBlog.com, February 27, 2017, https://youtube.googleblog.com/2017/02/you-know-whats-cool-billion-hours.html.
[52] George Chalhoub, "How much do YouTubers make when each of their videos get 50k, 100k, 500k, 1m, and 1.5m views? What about even more than that?," Quora.com, January 18, 2019, https://www.quora.com/How-much-do-YouTubers-make-when-each-of-their-videos-get-50k-100k-500k-1m-and-1-5m-views.
[53] "Larry Kosilla Matt Farah Car Detailing," *Ammo NYC*, August 3, 2012, https://www.youtube.com/watch?v=se0Xd2bwZ6U.
[54] "4400-Mile 1983 DeLorean DMC-12 5-Speed," *BringATrailer.com*, June 8, 2016, https://bringatrailer.com/listing/1983-delorean-dmc-12/.
[55] "Getting to Know Matt Farah," *Gears and Gasoline*, May 16, 2017, https://www.youtube.com/watch?v=EvIOBukMQHg.

[56] John Neff, "Engine power has increased 112% since 1980... and other fun facts about the Horsepower Wars," *Autoblog.com*, May 25, 2010, https://www.autoblog.com/2010/05/25/horsepower-has-increased-112-since-1980-and-other-fun-facts/.
[57] Robb Pritchard, "Before The 959 Porsche Dominated The Dakar With The 953, The First '911 4×4'," *Petrolicious.com*, March 2, 2018, https://petrolicious.com/articles/before-the-959-porsche-tackled-the-dakar-rally-with-this-911-4x4.
[58] "Safari auction results," *BringATrailer.com*, https://bringatrailer.com/search/safari/.
[59] Jonathan Ingram, "The 'Ring prepares Leh Keen for Le Mans," *Motorsport.com*, June 6, 2019, https://us.motorsport.com/endurance/news/the-ring-prepares-leh-keen-for-le-mans/2446816/.
[60] "Porsche 911 Safari Is Filthy Fun," *The Drive*, October 18, 2016, https://www.youtube.com/watch?v=LWNgs0mvoew.
[61] Jeff Peek, "The hottest 25 collector cars this summer (2018 edition)," *Hagerty.com*, August 1, 2018, https://www.hagerty.com/articles-videos/articles/2018/08/01/hottest-collector-cars-of-summer-2018.
[62] Rick Carey, "The Killer (Group) Bees are coming!," *Hagerty.com*, April 4, 2018, https://www.hagerty.com/articles-videos/articles/2018/04/04/values-of-group-b-rally-cars.
[63] "Lüftgekuhlt Pre-Party Tickets," Petersen Automotive Museum, https://petersentickets.org/products/luftgekuhlt?variant=3340357730328.
[64] "Lüftgekuhlt Book," *Luftbook.com*, https://www.luftbook.com/.
[65] Tara Hurlin, "Breaking Records at #Gridlife Midwest 2018," *DrivingLine.com*, June 25, 2018, https://www.drivingline.com/articles/breaking-records-at-gridlife-2018/.
[66] Bradley Brownell, "Gridlife Is The Bombastic Proof That Youth Car Culture Is Alive And Well," *Jalopnik.com*, September 8, 2017, https://jalopnik.com/gridlife-is-the-bombastic-proof-that-youth-car-culture-1801759050.
[67] "Wagner Selected to Head SCCA's Experiential Programs Department," *SCCA.com*, May 6, 2014, https://www.scca.com/articles/1992838-wagner-selected-to-head-sccaas-experiential-programs-department.
[68] Jack Baruth, "SCCA Time Trial Is Bringing Affordable Racing to Young Enthusiasts," *RoadAndTrack.com*, June 8, 2018, https://www.roadandtrack.com/motorsports/a21235515/scca-time-trial-is-bringing-affordable-racing-to-young-enthusiasts/.
[69] 24 Hours of LeMons, https://24hoursoflemons.com/.
[70] "Prices and Rules," 24 Hours of LeMons, https://24hoursoflemons.com/prices-rules/.
[71] @brojamotorsports, "A couple brewskis at the lazy liz and all the sudden the broja is a demolition match. If this is a preview of how the race will go, everyone's in for a rough road." *Instagram*, September 8, 2018, https://www.instagram.com/p/BndPSnnlPOb/?hl=en&taken-by=brojamotorsports.
[72] Jeff Olson, "Women in Indy 500 field no longer a talking point," *USAToday.com*, May 24, 2013, https://www.usatoday.com/story/sports/motor/indycar/2013/05/24/indy-500-four-women-in-the-field/2359161/.
[73] "Program History," *RevRacing.net*, https://revracing.net/program-history/.
[74] "NASCAR Diversity Internship Program welcomes largest class since inception," *NASCAR.com*, May 18, 2018, https://www.nascar.com/news-media/2018/05/18/nascar-diversity-internship-program-largest-class/.
[75] Pat DeCola, "NASCAR Next driver Hailie Deegan set for full K&N Pro Series slate in 2018," *NASCAR.com*, January 3, 2018, https://www.nascar.com/news-media/2018/01/02/nascar-next-driver-hailie-deegan-set-for-full-kn-pro-series-slate-in-2018/.

[76] "Lella Lombardi," Wikipedia.com, https://en.wikipedia.org/wiki/Lella_Lombardi.
[77] @Rob Harris, Rob Harris, "Racing driver @CarmenJorda speaking @CSM_Europe on F1: "It's not fair to be compared with men because we will never be on the same level," *Twitter*, October 11, 2017, https://twitter.com/RobHarris/status/918183010855456770.
[78] @CarmenJorda, Carmen Jorda, "I believe a women's F1 championship would give us the chance to achieve our dreams and compete on an equal footing - as in other sports.," *Twitter*, October 12, 2017, https://twitter.com/CarmenJorda/status/918428227969978368.
[79] @PippaMann, Pippa Mann, "She does know that @ChristinaRacing was just crowned @IMSA GTD Champion for second straight year... right? 😑 *Beats ahead against wall*," Twitter, October 12, 2017, https://twitter.com/PippaMann/status/918453295341101058.
[80] "Tatiana Calderon leads the way for women in F1 and motorsport," *TheWeek.com*, March 8, 2018, http://www.theweek.co.uk/formula-1/92160/tatiana-calderon-sauber-test-driver-women-in-f1-motorsport.
[81] Pippa Mann, "The Handmaid's Racing Series," *PippaMann.com*, June 19, 2017, http://www.pippamann.com/2017/06/19/the-handmaids-racing-series/.
[82] "Shea Holbrook," WSeries.com, https://wseries.com/drivers/shea-holbrook/.
[83] "Women on Track," *SCCAFoundation.com*, http://www.sccafoundation.com/women-on-track/.
[84] "Philadelphia Region Women Racers," *Facebook.com*, https://www.facebook.com/groups/phillywot/about/
[85] "Rankings," ProjectCarEsports.com, https://www.projectcarsesports.com/rankings.html.
[86] "GT Academy Winner Makes it to the Podium of the Le Mans," *Gran-Turismo.com*, June 17, 2011, https://www.gran-turismo.com/us/news/02_0005816.html.
[87] Nazvi Careem, "Virtual driver Enzo Bonito beats Formula E champion Luca di Grassi in one-on-one real race," *South China Morning Post*, January 23, 2019, https://www.scmp.com/sport/motorsport/article/2183300/virtual-driver-enzo-bonito-beats-formula-e-champion-luca-di-grassi.
[88] "2018 New Balance Pro Series Driver Standings," *F1esports.com*, https://f1esports.com/pro-series/2018.
[89] "Virtual Racers Go for Pro in the Second GT Academy National Finals Event," *usa.nissannews.com*, http://nissannews.com/en-US/nissan/usa/releases/virtual-racers-go-for-pro-in-the-2nd-gt-academy-national-finals-event?mode=print.
[90] "Forza Racing Championship Leaderboards," *ForzaRC.com*, https://forzarc.com/leaderboard.
[91] Isaac Forcella, "Every Driver and Team Competing at the ForzaRC Seattle Invitational," *FullThrottleMedia.com*, https://www.fullthrottlemedia.co.uk/article/forzarc-seattle-drivers-teams.
[92] *ProjectCarsEsports.com*, https://www.projectcarsesports.com/.
[93] Scott Mitchell, "McLaren signs winner of World's Fastest Gamer as F1 sim driver," *autosport.com*, https://www.autosport.com/gaming/news/133191/mclaren-signs-esports-winner-as-f1-sim-driver.
[94] "ForzaRC 2018 Series 1 Playoffs - Day 2," *Forza Racing Championship on YouTube.com*, https://www.youtube.com/watch?v=99Y28Y8kEcU&t=7708s.
[95] "Historic Districts, Planning Districts and Multi-Property Resources – 02/26/13," Los Angeles Historic Resources Society, *lacity.org*, http://preservation.lacity.org/files/Encino-Tarzana Districts.pdf.
[96] George P. Edmonston Jr., "OAC's king of the stunt card," *GazetteTimes.com*, https://www.gazettetimes.com/oac-s-king-of-the-stunt-card/article_61b8ddca-5247-5d2b-bd3a-e7732cf67c08.html.

[97] James Ricci, "Vestige of Idyllic Life Still Bears Fruit," *latimes.com*, August 29, 1998, http://articles.latimes.com/1998/aug/29/local/me-17623.

[98] Edward J. Boyer, "Lindley Bothwell : USC's 'Mr. B,' Yell, Song Girl Coach, Dies," *latimes.com*, June 21, 1986, http://articles.latimes.com/1986-06-21/news/mn-19671_1_usc-song.

[99] "The Bothwell Collection," *bonhams.com*, https://images1.bonhams.com/original?src=Images/live/2017-10/25/S-24733-0-2.pdf.

[100] Jason Torchinsky, "Here's What DOHC Means And Why It Matters," *jalopnik.com*, February 18, 2018, https://jalopnik.com/heres-what-dohc-means-and-why-it-matters-1823401676.

[101] "The Bothwell Collection, *bonhams.com*, https://www.bonhams.com/auctions/24733/.

[102] "Bothwell Collection Bonhams Auction," *BlacktopTV* on *YouTube.com*, https://www.youtube.com/watch?v=d-wsuSsFYgg.

[103] Daniel Indiviglio, "The Economic Recovery Marched Slowly Forward in 2010," *theatlantic.com*, December 31, 2010, https://www.theatlantic.com/business/archive/2010/12/the-economic-recovery-marched-slowly-forward-in-2010/68719/.

[104] Josh Zumbrun, "Not Just the 1%: The Upper Middle Class Is Larger and Richer Than Ever," *wsj.com*, June 21, 2016, https://blogs.wsj.com/economics/2016/06/21/not-just-the-1-the-upper-middle-class-is-larger-and-richer-than-ever/.

[105] Albert Roxas, "The Rise of the Air-Cooled: Porsche 930/964/993," *drivingline.com*, October 9, 2014, https://www.drivingline.com/articles/the-rise-of-the-air-cooled-porsche-930964993/.

[106] Joe Breeze, "Is it too late to buy a Porsche 911 Carrera RS 2.7?", *classicdriver.com*, November 14, 2014, https://www.classicdriver.com/en/article/cars/it-too-late-buy-porsche-911-carrera-rs-27.

[107] Steve Statham, "Starting Line: Welcome to the classic car hobby – there's room for everyone," *barrett-jackson.com*, March 16, 2017, http://www.barrett-jackson.com/Media/Home/Reader/barrett-jackson-starting-car-collecting-millennials/.

[108] "Embracing Change: Younger generations are finding much to like about Barrett-Jackson auctions," *barrett-jackson.com*, August 22, 2017, http://www.barrett-jackson.com/Media/Home/Reader/barrett-jackson-millennials-collector-car-hobby/.

[109] Larry Edsall, "Hagerty offers Arizona auction coverage, car by car as they cross block," *journal.classiccars.com*, January 19, 2018, https://journal.classiccars.com/2018/01/19/hagerty-offers-arizona-auction-coverage-car-car-cross-block/.

[110] "Lot #158 1994 Toyota Supra Turbo Lift-Back," *barrett-jackson.com*, https://www.barrett-jackson.com/Events/Event/Details/1994-TOYOTA-SUPRA-TURBO-LIFT-BACK-188589.

[111] Parker Leavitt, "Millennials growing force at Barrett-Jackson car auction," *freep.com*, January 21, 2017, https://www.freep.com/story/money/nation-now/2017/01/21/millennials-growing-force-barrett-jackson-car-auction/96913638/.

[112] "Lot #681 1971 Chevrolet Custom K5 Blazer 4x4," *barrett-jackson.com*, https://www.barrett-jackson.com/Events/Event/Details/1971-CHEVROLET-CUSTOM-K5-BLAZER-4X4-205901.

[113] Larry Edsall, "It's true: Hagerty survey finds millennials like to drive," *journal.classiccars.com*, June 27, 2018, https://journal.classiccars.com/2018/06/27/its-true-hagerty-survey-finds-millennials-like-to-drive/.
[114] Mike Guilfoyle, "Gen Xers and millennials are ready to carry the collectible-car torch," *hagerty.com*, July 24, 2018, https://www.hagerty.com/articles-videos/articles/2018/07/24/gen-x-and-millenials-are-ready-to-carry-the-collectible-car-torch.
[115] "About," *bringatrailer.com*, https://bringatrailer.com/about/.
[116] "1989 Nissan Skyline GT-R," *bringatrailer.com*, https://bringatrailer.com/listing/1991-nissan-skyline-gt-r-7/.
[117] "1991 Nissan Skyline GT-R," *bringatrailer.com*, https://bringatrailer.com/listing/1991-nissan-skyline-gt-r-9/.
[118] "95-Mile 2015 Ferrari LaFerrari," *bringatrailer.com*, https://bringatrailer.com/listing/2015-ferrari-laferrari/
[119] "Renault R5 Turbo," *bringatrailer.com*, https://bringatrailer.com/renault/r5-turbo/
[120] "Lancia Delta," *bringatrailer.com*, https://bringatrailer.com/lancia/delta/
[121] "Bonhams Scottsdale 2018 – Auction Results," *sportscardigest.com*, January 22, 2018, http://www.sportscardigest.com/bonhams-scottsdale-2018-auction-results/.
[122] Rick Carey, "The Killer (Group) Bees are coming!," hagerty.com, April 4, 2018, https://www.hagerty.com/articles-videos/articles/2018/04/04/values-of-group-b-rally-cars.
[123] "RM Sotheby's Brings A 'Youngtimer' Dream Garage To Auction In 2019," *rmsothebys.com*, December 4, 2018, https://rmsothebys.com/en/home/media-center/press-releases/19_youngtimer-dream-garage/736401.
[124] "Cars Sold," *thecultivatedcollector.com*, https://thecultivatedcollector.com/automobile-inventory/sold/
[125] "1962 Aston Martin Series IV DB4," *thecultivatedcollector.com*, https://thecultivatedcollector.com/automobile-inventory/for-sale/1962-aston-martin-series-iv-db4/
[126] "1961 Lancia Appia Sport Zagato," *thecultivatedcollector.com*, https://thecultivatedcollector.com/automobile-inventory/for-sale/1961-lancia-appia-sport-zagato/.
[127] "1987 Sierra RS Cosworth," *thecultivatedcollector.com*, https://thecultivatedcollector.com/automobile-inventory/for-sale/sierra-rs-cosworth/.
[128] "1989 BMW E30 M3 Convertible," *goodingco.com*, https://www.goodingco.com/vehicle/1989-bmw-e30-m3-convertible/.
[129] "1991 BMW E30 M3 Convertible," *goodingco.com*, https://www.goodingco.com/vehicle/1991-bmw-e30-m3-convertible/.
[130] "1989 BMW M3 Coupe," *bonhams.com*, https://www.bonhams.com/auctions/22792/lot/18/.
[131] "35K-Mile 1989 BMW M3," *bringatrailer.com*, https://bringatrailer.com/listing/1989-bmw-m3-26/.
[132] Taylor, James. *BMW M3: The Complete Story*. The Crowood Press, 2014.
[133] "BMW M3 (E30) specs," *fastestlaps.com*, http://fastestlaps.com/models/bmw-m3-e30.
[134] Dino Dalle Carbonare, "DTM Aspirations: The Clever 190E 2.3-16," *speedhunters.com*, March 17, 2015, http://www.speedhunters.com/2015/03/clever-mercedes-benz-190e-cosworth/.
[135] Terry Shea, "The Driver's Benz – 1985-'88 Mercedes-Benz 190E 2.3-16," *hemmings.com*, April 2017, https://www.hemmings.com/magazine/hsx/2017/04/The-Driver-s-Benz---1985--88-Mercedes-Benz-190E-2-3-16/3750727.html.
[136] 2016 DTM. BMW Motorsport Media Information. [pdf]

[137] "1987: Year of the Juniors," *dtm.com*, https://www.dtm.com/en/history/1987-season.
[138] Aaron Bayne, "BMW M3: History in Rally," automoblog.net, March 2, 2015, https://www.automoblog.net/2015/03/02/bmw-m3-history-rally/.
[139] Adam Davis, "40 years of BMW 3 Series: The M3 World Rally Car," motoring.com.au, October 24, 2015, https://www.motoring.com.au/40-years-of-bmw-3-series-the-m3-world-rally-car-54723/.
[140] Bob Sorokanich, "Whoa, the E30 BMW M3 Made a Kick-Ass Rally Car," *roadandtrack.com*, August 5, 2016, https://www.roadandtrack.com/motorsports/videos/a30293/whoa-the-e30-bmw-m3-made-a-kick-ass-rally-car/.
[141] "Throw-back to maiden Nordschleife victory: Historic livery for BMW Team Schnitzer BMW M6 GT3," *bmw-motorsport.com*, January 25, 2017, https://www.bmw-motorsport.com/en/topics/magazine-article-pool/throw-back-to-maiden-nordschleife-victory:-historic-livery-for-bmw-team-schnitzer-bmw-m6-gt3.html.
[142] Sam Sheehan, "Winning cars of the Spa 24 Hours," *evo.co.uk*, July 23, 2015, http://www.evo.co.uk/features/16390/winning-cars-of-the-spa-24-hours/page/0/1.
[143] "All Results of Eric van de Poele," *racingsportscars.com*, https://www.racingsportscars.com/driver/results/Eric-van de Poele-B.html.
[144] "1989 BMW M3 Johnny Cecotto Edition," *enthusiastauto.com*, http://enthusiastauto.com/qsearch/?id=5511&form_display=51.
[145] "BMW E46 M3," *bringatrailer.com*, https://bringatrailer.com/bmw/e46-m3/.
[146] "FCA US Reports 2016 December and Full-year U.S. Sales," *media.fcanorthamerica.com*, January 4, 2017, https://media.fcanorthamerica.com/newsrelease.do?id=18073. "FCA US LLC Sales Summary December 2017," *media.fcanorthamerica.com*, January 3, 2018, https://media.fcanorthamerica.com/newsrelease.do?id=18762 [pdf]. "FCA US LLC Sales Summary December 2018," *media.fcanorthamerica.com*, January 3, 2019, https://media.fcanorthamerica.com/newsrelease.do?id=20509&mid=1 [pdf].
[147] Donn Anderson, "BMW's iconic M3," *themotorhood.com*, December 16, 2016, http://www.themotorhood.com/themotorhood/2016/9/11/bmws-iconic-m3.
[148] Andrew Newton, "Hagerty Vehicle Rating Bottom 25: Classic American cars, British sports cars, and a few Ferraris lag behind," *hagerty.com*, February 20, 2018, https://www.hagerty.com/articles-videos/articles/2018/02/20/hvr-bottom-25-feb-2018.
[149] "5. Rheinpokal Rennen," *touringcarracing.net*, http://touringcarracing.net/Races/1970 Rheinpokal.html.
[150] Thomas Ammerschläger, "Making the Cologne Capri quicker," automobilsport-magazin.de, May 12, 2014, https://www.automobilsport-magazin.de/en/back-issues/issue/articles/issue-03.html.
[151] "Ford Super-Capri," *72stagpower.com*, https://www.72stagpower.com/en/the-legends/ford-super-capri/.
[152] Taylor, James. *BMW M3: The Complete Story*. The Crowood Press, 2014.
[153] "The BMW M3 (E30) film. Everything about the first BMW M3 generation.," *BMW* on *YouTube.com*, December 17, 2015, https://www.youtube.com/watch?v=X2gUrmPvmBA.
[154] "ArtCenter at a Glance," *artcenter.edu*, http://www.artcenter.edu/about/get-to-know-artcenter/artcenter-at-a-glance.html.
[155] "Tuition and Aid," *artcenter.edu*, http://www.artcenter.edu/admissions/tuition-and-aid/tuition-and-fees/tuition.html.
[156] "HILLSIDE CAMPUS: The 30th Anniversary of Art Center's move to Pasadena," *artcenter.edu*, http://www2.artcenter.edu/archives/hillside/construction6.html.

[157] "How McLaren Automotive uses virtual reality to design its sportscars and supercars," McLaren Automotive on youtube.com, March 22, 2018, https://www.youtube.com/watch?v=mWaQfjEJIMQ.
[158] Chitra Sethi, "Manufacturing Cars with Virtual Reality," asme.org, March 2, 2017, https://www.asme.org/engineering-topics/articles/manufacturing-design/manufacturing-cars-with-virtual-reality.
[159] "Status Report: Flexing muscle," *iihs.org*, May 24, 2016, http://www.iihs.org/iihs/sr/statusreport/article/51/5/2.
[160] "Status Report: Tough test for pickups," *iihs.org*, April 12, 2016, http://www.iihs.org/iihs/sr/statusreport/article/51/4/3.
[161] "Status Report: Flexing muscle," *iihs.org*, May 24, 2016, http://www.iihs.org/iihs/sr/statusreport/article/51/5/2.
[162] "John Force explosion then crashed into Jonnie Lindberg," *Andy Roberts* on *YouTube.com*, February 25, 2018, https://www.youtube.com/watch?v=woUlxpdZxgQ.
[163] "BCRA & USAC Midgets MAIN 7-15-17 Petaluma Speedway," *qzimr* on *YouTube.com*, July 17, 2017, https://www.youtube.com/watch?v=_YgUQZwFLM0.
[164] "Findings: Dan Wheldon's head hit post," *espn.com*, December 15, 2011, https://www.espn.com/racing/indycar/story/_/id/7355694/dan-wheldon-head-hit-fence-post-indycar-says-report-fatal-crash.
[165] "The INDYCAR Earpiece Sensor System," *indycar.com*, https://www.indycar.com/Fan-Info/INDYCAR-101/The-Drivers/Earpiece.
[166] Curt Cavin, "Investigation: Dan Wheldon died when head hit fence post," *usatoday30.usatoday.com*, December 15, 2011, http://usatoday30.usatoday.com/sports/motor/indycar/story/2011-12-15/dan-wheldon-death-investigation/51963662/1.
[167] Bruce Martin, "After Wheldon's death, safety is priority in 2012 IndyCar Series," *si.com*, March 23, 2012, https://www.si.com/racing/2012/03/23/indycar-safety.
[168] John Oreovicz, "New Indy car still needs work," espn.com, December 21, 2011, http://www.espn.com/racing/indycar/story/_/id/7375857/indycar-new-dallara-chassis-proving-difficult-sort-out.
[169] "Opticor Advanced Transparency Material," *ppgaerospace.com*, http://www.ppgaerospace.com/getdoc/14c02e46-c994-4621-8ac2-36d5a18227a4/Opticor-Advanced-Transparency-Material.aspx.
[170] Mark Robinson, "Dixon, Indycar pleased with windscreen prototype's first track test," *indycar.com*, February 9, 2018, https://www.indycar.com/News/2018/02/02-09-Windscreen-test-Phoenix.
[171] Karen Travers, Mark Flamini, Jessica Small, "10 Years Later: How Dale Earnhardt's Death at Daytona 500 Changed NASCAR," *abcnews.go.com*, February 19, 2010, https://abcnews.go.com/Politics/nascar-ten-years-earnhardts-death-nascars-changed-sport/story?id=12949157.
[172] John Dorfman, "Carlo Bugatti: Furnishing a Fantasy," *artandantiquesmag.com*, May 2015, http://www.artandantiquesmag.com/2015/05/carlo-bugatti-designs/.
[173] Richard Micheal Owen, "1936 Bugatti Type 57SC Atlantic," *supercars.net*, March 10, 2016, https://www.supercars.net/blog/1936-bugatti-type-57sc-atlantic/.
[174] "The Bugatti Type 57 SC Atlantic - A Style Icon," *bugatti.com*, February 22, 2019, https://www.bugatti.com/media/news/2019/the-bugatti-type-57-sc-atlantic-a-style-icon/.
[175] "Bugatti Atlantic #3: An important car reappears," *motorsportsmarketingresources.com*, http://www.motorsportsmarketingresources.com/short-stories/mmr-stories/bugatti-atlantic-3-an-important-car-reappears.html.

[176] "Peter Mullin Automotive Museum Foundation," *projects.propublica.org*, https://projects.propublica.org/nonprofits/organizations/201728744.
[177] "1937 Talbot-Lago T150-C SS 'Goutte d'Eau' Coupé by Figoni et Falaschi," *rmsothebys.com*, May 2017, http://www.rmsothebys.com/en/auctions/VE17/Villa-Erba/lots/r103-1937-talbot-lago-t150-c-ss-goutte-d-eau-coupé-by-figoni-et-falaschi/416702.
[178] "Talbot-Lago," *Wikipedia.com*, https://en.wikipedia.org/wiki/Talbot-Lago.
[179] "1938 Talbot-Lago T150-C SS Teardrop Coupé by Figoni et Falaschi," *rmsothebys.com*, May 2011, https://rmsothebys.com/en/auctions/VE11/Villa-d%27Este/lots/r109-1938-talbot-lago-t150-c-ss-teardrop-coupé-by-figoni-et-falaschi/186893.

www.ingramcontent.com/pod-product-compliance
Lightning Source LLC
LaVergne TN
LVHW090823290525
812111LV00014B/52
* 9 7 8 0 5 7 8 5 4 9 7 0 5 *